MAKE ME LIKE YOU, LORD

COLLEEN TOWNSEND EVANS

MAKE ME LIKE YOU, LORD

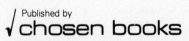

Published by
chosen books

FLEMING H. REVELL COMPANY
OLD TAPPAN, NEW JERSEY

The poem by Luci Shaw on pp. 29–30 is reprinted from *The Secret Trees* © 1976 by Luci Shaw and used by permission of Harold Shaw Publishers.

The poem on pages 158–159, from *Toward Jerusalem* by Amy Carmichael © 1936 Dohnavur Fellowship, Fort Wayne, Pa.: Christian Literature Crusade, is used by permission.

Unless otherwise noted, Scripture texts are from the Holy Bible, New International Version, copyright © 1973, 1978, 1984 International Bible Society. Used by permission of Zondervan Bible Publishers.

Library of Congress Cataloging-in-Publication Data

Evans, Colleen Townsend.
    Make me like you, Lord / by Colleen Townsend Evans.
      p. cm.
    Bibliography: p.
    ISBN 0-8007-9153-3
    1. Christian life—Presbyterian authors. 2. Evans, Colleen Townsend. I. Title.
    BV4501.2.E86   1989
    248.4'851—dc20   89-15695
                                             CIP

A Chosen Book
Copyright © 1989 by Colleen Townsend Evans

Chosen Books are published by
Fleming H. Revell Company
Old Tappan, New Jersey
Printed in the United States of America

— For Sam and Vicky Hines —
who are continually growing
in the likeness of Jesus
and who continually bless
our lives with the
friendship we share.

Contents

Introduction

Although this is a book on becoming like Jesus, it is definitely not a how-to book.

For the fact is that you cannot by your own effort, your own skill, make yourself more like the Master. There is nothing you can *do* to become like Him because He is the One who does the work. Your job and mine, as we will see, is to respond.

Yet, strangely, for us human beings who so want to stay in control, this is not one bit easy. The very first step in responding to Christ in you is to recognize His call. Is there a dull feeling of dissatisfaction inside you? An emotional or spiritual ache? Your life may be busy, even productive. On the surface all seems well—no one would suspect anything awry. But on the level of awareness only you and God are privy to, you know something is not right.

I wonder if the reason for your restlessness may be that you are not growing. I ask this because I have been going through this same restlessness myself over the last couple of years, and I have had to be reminded—all over again—that growth is central to God's plan for my life.

The truth is, you and I *should* ache with holy dissatisfaction when growth is not taking place. Not growth for growth's sake and not just any kind of growth! For those of us who have made a conscious commitment of our lives to Jesus Christ, growth is meant to take us in a very specific direction.

Mahatma Gandhi said to one of his Christian friends: "I like your Christ—but I don't like your Christians. They are so *unlike* your Christ."

In that scathing statement Gandhi revealed our need and pointed us to our goal. No matter how busy or productive we are, no matter how many achievements we gather in our baskets, if we are not becoming more like Jesus we are not growing according to God's plan.

So this is not a book for achievers; it is for the "poor in spirit"—those who know their need and look eagerly for direction.

It is for hungry, thirsty beginners who want more of God in their lives.

It is for mature Christians who have somehow gotten off the track and need to go back to the basics of the faith.

It is for those who are discouraged—wary of straining and trying so hard to be religious.

It is for those who are ready to open themselves to the Spirit's work—and to allow God to change them from the inside out.

In short, this is a book for people in process: those who are ready to experience the joy and cost of growing into the likeness of Jesus.

This is my journey. I hope you will join me.

Colleen Townsend Evans

MAKE ME LIKE LIKE YOU, LORD

1
Made to Grow

It was April and Washington, D.C., was in the process of bursting forth. If I live to be one hundred I will never get over the outrageous beauty that envelops the capital in the spring. New blossoms and green everywhere!

Louie, my husband, who is pastor of the National Presbyterian Church, and I were walking out of the church building toward the parking lot, with the warmth of the spring afternoon washing pleasantly over us, when we spotted our friend Chico Rodriguez. Chief groundskeeper of the church at that time, Chico cared for everything that grew on the campus and we wanted to thank him for our visual feast.

But Chico was in no mood to accept our kudos. He fumed and pointed to his prized holly trees. He had carefully pruned them over the years into a perfect conical shape, making an elegant frieze around the perimeter of the sanctuary. But conical they were no longer. While Chico was on extended sick leave, the temporary landscape contractor had cut them back into prosaic spherical shapes. Their elegance had vanished!

Chico was furious. "It will take me years to change them back. You understand how it works? I can only shape them as they grow—and growth takes a *looooong* time," he sputtered.

Louie sympathized with his frustration and gave him

some deserved affirmation. Soon we were on our way, but, driving home in our blue Omega, Louie was unusually quiet. I could tell his active mind was working on something, so I kept silent all the way into the city. Just as we passed the Capitol and drove into the Southeast neighborhood where we live, the silence was broken.

"Ah ha!" Louie exclaimed. "That's it! God can mold a church only when its people are growing."

Louie had often stated that if a congregation is not growing and changing constantly—*Semper reformanda** in the words of the Reformers—it is in trouble. "I've been trying to *preach* renewal into being and to program it like an engineer," he continued. "But that's not how it happens."

Louie found a place to park near the tall, narrow, gray row house we call home, but we stayed in our car, talking.

"The only way a church is going to know God's continual renewal is through continual growth. And at God's pace, not ours. As we grow, then God can shape us and transform us into the people He means for us to be."

WE ARE MADE FOR GROWTH

Yes, God had a sermon for Louie in Chico's message about growing and shaping. And God had a lesson for me as well. He could only shape me, transform me, to the extent of *my* growth!

Long after we finally climbed out of our car and went inside that Sunday, I found myself captivated by the concept of growth—specifically as it relates to our spiritual lives.

"Growth is our destiny, written into blood and tissue and

---

* Always being reformed.

nerve and cell and organ—written into us," said E. Stanley Jones, one of the Christian giants of this century.

Growth and transformation are built into our spiritual DNA! God created us this way, and while we may stifle the urge within us, it will not go away. In fact, our desire to grow—to find spiritual fulfillment—is so deep, it is like marrow in our bones.

Our physical bodies will slow down, of course. We accept—rather reluctantly!—their limits. But not so the spirit. Deep within us we somehow know the spirit is destined to soar. By growing it can be transformed into something beyond our understanding. So we humans, made in the image of God, reach out, press on, stretch, yearn, and sometimes literally ache for growth and transformation. And as Christians we come to recognize that ache as a desire to grow spiritually into the likeness of Jesus.

Not that the yearning is constant: Sometimes it lies fallow, just under the surface of consciousness. Then without warning it springs to life and a holy dissatisfaction with things as they are begins to churn around inside.

The goal of becoming like Him is before us and unless we are moving toward it nothing else can bring true satisfaction.

Knowing that we are all created for growth, I have been eager over the past months for a new work of God in my life. Each season has possessed its own blend of busyness and stress. But the immediate past season has had dimensions all its own. In addition to the home, church, and community involvements I normally have, there were marriages and births, tender, rich times of joy and emotion within our family circle. And there were new challenges—specifically, the co-chairing of The Greater Washington Billy Graham Crusade, which took more than a year of planning and preparation. It thrilled me to be part of the coming together of our city as people across all lines were united in the Person of Jesus Christ.

Then, having come to the end of this incredibly rich but very busy and demanding season of activity, I found myself with a sudden spiritual hunger. My soul felt weary and barren from that long stretch of busyness and it was calling for attention. I *had* to listen.

And when I did, I heard quiet but very clear orders from above to allow God the time and space to do a new work in my life.

GETTING STARTED

While we are made to grow into the likeness of Jesus, that growth doesn't come without struggle. For instance, following my new orders was not easy, for it meant pulling away from worthwhile activities. It meant saying no to people I cared about deeply—friends and colleagues who had legitimate agendas for my time and energy.

But it was not just other people who made it difficult to get started. I waged a battle with guilt and with the fear that taking time off would mean becoming unproductive for the Lord. Which made me realize all over again what a job the world has done on most of us. We read the Gospels through lenses shaped by our cultural conditioning. And so we link growth—even our growth in Christ—with production and busyness.

Consider how much of the world's teaching we have absorbed into the fabric of our minds:

• "Growing people are busy people," we hear. They are always on the move. Their datebooks are so jammed they must sign up for seminars on managing time.

• "Growing people are in touch with the times." They watch the indicators—"Gallup poll Christians," one friend calls them.

• "Growing people," the world says, "are achievers who are rewarded with money, power, and influence."

• And, perhaps most seductive of all, the world tells us that "growth can be quantified, measured, recorded." There is a bottom line for growth that the world honors. And, whether we want to acknowledge it or not, most Christians do, too.

One observer of the Christian scene noted that the Puritans lived as if they had swallowed gyroscopes. Their bearings were inside them because of their deep inner calling. Modern Christians too often live as if they swallowed Gallup polls, looking around for approval, affirmation, confirmation . . . guidelines as to where they should be and what they should be following.

I have the privilege of serving several Christian ministries—good ministries that I believe in or I wouldn't be there. At a recent board meeting of a new and much-needed outreach ministry, however, I had some rather unsettling feelings.

We were dealing with compensation and I was suddenly struck by the thought that, except for the fact that the meeting was opened in prayer, we could have been almost any secular enterprise. The way we evaluated success and rewarded it was virtually the same as any non-Christian institution. I expressed my uneasiness. There were others who agreed. The way we came to our conclusions that day, however, was not altered. Our cultural conditioning had been thorough.

It was against this subtle conditioning by our society that I had to battle when I sensed my orders from God. The message to me was clear. I was not to *do* more, *try* harder, or *get busier*. Instead I was to pull back, to be silent and listen. I was to make space for growth.

MY ROCKING CHAIR RETREAT

The adventure began simply enough. I didn't cloister myself. I didn't make an announcement. Family responsibilities were met, friends were seen, long-time commitments kept. But nothing new was taken on. Each day I simply tried to put aside as much time as I could for basic spiritual disciplines . . . the things that feed and nourish.

It helps me to have a place to do this kind of earnest business with God. For me that place is my old, three-times slip-covered rocking chair that sits in my small sitting room/ study. In other years in other places, I have gone to that chair to do my "quiet things"—to nurse our babies, to read, and to listen for God's voice. And many times when I have felt special needs I have gone to my chair in the middle of the night, as to a trusted friend, and kneeling by its side, put my head in its faded, comfortable lap, and wept my heart out to the Lord.

So it was natural that I should go to my holy place now. There I began a new study of the Gospels—soaking (what Louie calls my "marinating process") in the life of Jesus. I also started digging into the must-read books that had gathered over the months on the chair side table.

And of course I prayed. In fact, prayer became a much more central part of every 24 hours as I responded to those middle-of-the-night nudges to slip out of bed, go to my chair, and talk to God. On numerous occasions dawn filled the room through the skylight above the chair—a very unusual thing for me to witness since I am constitutionally opposed to early risings!

I also began the habit of stopping during the day to snatch small opportunities to talk to God wherever I was, or simply to affirm His presence in my life. I was surprised at how many such opportunities there were, once I began watching for them.

Then there were the hours of quiet waiting. I was weary of asking God to bless *my* plans. I wanted so much to know what *He* willed. I wanted to know where *He* meant to prune activities from my schedule, what new obedience *He* meant for me to follow in order to stretch and grow.

And so I waited and I listened. There was only one voice I wanted to hear, and it didn't seem to be in a hurry to speak.

Days and weeks passed.

There was no clear voice.

But slowly, almost imperceptibly, I began to be aware of the stirring of new growth. The spiritual barrenness I had experienced began to fade, as though a gentle breeze was wafting it away.

And as I read and reread the Gospels—those biblical accounts of Jesus' life on earth—I felt refreshed by the clear way they presented Jesus, who He was, what He came to do, and how He related to all kinds of people. It was deeply satisfying to sense a closeness to Him again, a bit like getting back in step with a trusted friend who had always been there for me, but from whom I had momentarily wandered.

Then one quiet afternoon, the voice I had been waiting for spoke clearly to my heart.

I was reading the Gospel of Matthew—lingering long in the first chapter after all the "begats." I had pictured Jesus calling the first disciples to Himself. I had listened to Him teach as His new friends sat around Him on the side of the mountain—and in my mind I saw the crowds gather and grow as He healed people and explained the nature of His Father's Kingdom.

Then I came to chapter 10. Jesus was giving His disciples instructions for their new calling. And there, in the midst of His charge to them, He makes an incredible statement: "It is enough for the disciple to be *like* his teacher, and the servant *like* his master" (verse 25, RSV, emphasis added.).

I reached for my study Bible and found that the word *enough* as Jesus used it meant "satiated, full to overflowing." There could be nothing more than *enough.*

As I pondered the meaning of those words I began to sense a flicker of insight. Then the wind of the Spirit blew the flicker into flame and its light flooded my heart with an "ah ha" kind of understanding. In that moment I knew that we will never achieve the perfect likeness of Jesus as long as we are alive on this earth. Of course not! Jesus is God. We will not be like Him until we experience physical death and are with Him in that mysterious face-to-face encounter we read about in Scripture (1 John 3:2).

On the other hand, I sensed that we were to be *shaped* ever more toward His likeness even here on earth. This is the desire of God's heart. If we allow Him to do His work in us, we are moving in the direction of His likeness. We are being made more like Him. And to want to be like Jesus is not presumptuous . . . it is yielding to His plan and His dream for our lives.

"It is enough," Jesus said, "for the servant to be *like* his master."

BEING TRANSFORMED ACCORDING TO GOD'S PLAN

As I sat in the afterglow of that "ah ha" moment, I thought again how different being transformed according to God's design is from the way our culture has conditioned us to go. When Christlikeness is our goal, there will be no charts to tell us we are doing well. Transformation may be invisible to anyone but God. Indeed we may find that growth occurs most when we are least aware it is happening. And while the world shouts, "Busy, busy, run, run," our Lord whispers, "Peace, be still," and lets us know that hurrying won't help us get to our goals any faster. In fact, straining and striving will only get in the way.

I recalled the words of George MacDonald, "It takes a long time to finish the new creation of redemption," and I thought again of Chico and those holly bushes in front of the church. "Growth takes a looooong time!"

And I knew it was true.

While the understanding that we were created to grow in the likeness of Jesus can be ours in a moment, the re-shaping of our lives and the working out of God's dream will take a lifetime. It is a journey and Jesus is saying to us, just as truly as He said to the first disciples, "Come follow Me. It will not be an easy road, but I will be there to help you over the rough places. It may be a long road, but I will keep you company all the way."

In his second letter to the Corinthians, Paul reminds us that when Moses came down from Mt. Sinai he was transformed, yet he was not aware that "his face shone." But it did shine because he had been with God! And so it can be for us.

As we walk the same road with Jesus and open our lives to Him; as we "reflect the Lord's glory" (2 Corinthians 3:18), experience His love and forgiveness; as we make His unselfishness our example—we too will be influenced and changed.

For there is no way we can be in His presence and stay the same. We will become people reshaped and changed from the inside out. When that happens, the miracle of transformation has begun and His likeness has begun to be formed in our lives.

Question Ideas

1. Is there an eagerness, perhaps even a restlessness within you because of your need and desire to grow spiritually?

2. If so, how has the world influenced the way you think about and measure growth?

3. How do you feel about Jesus' statement in Matthew 10: "It is enough for the disciple to be *like* his teacher, and the servant *like* his Master"?

4. What might you do to begin the "holy process" of growing in the likeness of Jesus?

2

The Secret of Growth

It was a Sunday afternoon in December a number of years ago. The California sun was shining and Louie and I and our four children had just come home from a long morning at the La Jolla Presbyterian Church where Louie was pastor. After lunch everyone wandered off to his or her own quiet corner of our house overlooking the ocean. Our family had lived in La Jolla for a decade. We thoroughly enjoyed our life and work in California . . . and most of all the good people with whom we served at the church.

The children were reading or snoozing and I was still puttering around in the kitchen when the phone rang. Louie and I picked up different receivers at the same time and a man's voice, assured and firm on the other end of the line, said:

"Dr. and Mrs. Evans, I'm glad you're both on the line, because what I have to say is important. You will need to be very prayerful about your response."

Do I need to say that his next words had our *full* attention? And rightly so, for that phone call changed the direction of our lives. A few months later our family moved from California to Washington, D.C., to serve in new ways to a new people in a new place.

When Jesus walked this earth teaching and preaching, He had His ways of commanding people's attention when He was about to ask for a response that would change the direction of their lives. Sometimes He began a teaching by saying, "Verily, verily" or "Truly, truly I say unto you," or, loosely translated, "Listen—all of you—what I am about to say is important and I want you to *really* hear Me."

As I seek to unravel the secret of growing in the likeness of Jesus, I have an urge to command your attention in the same way. I want to color this section in red, sprinkle it with exclamation points, do anything I can to underscore the truth I am asking God to communicate through this chapter. I want to celebrate with you the meaning of God's mysterious secret for our lives, and it is this: "This mystery, which is Christ *in* you, the hope of glory" (Colossians 1:27, emphasis added).

Jesus wants to be born in us. He wants to live His life *through* you and me. This is God's way to enable us to live the Christian life—a life that is utterly impossible otherwise. And this is the only way we can hope to grow in the likeness of Jesus. The theme of this chapter is God doing in and through us what we could never do for ourselves.

When this secret began to be real to me it made such an astonishing difference that it was akin to snuffing out a candle because dawn had broken. The candle, which had seemed so bright in the night, faded to nothing in the face of the sun. In the same way the burden and strain of trying to live the Christian life in my own strength was gone at last.

STOP STRIVING—START TRUSTING

Three of my favorite Christian writers, men I will be referring to often, are E. Stanley Jones, Andrew Murray, and Oswald Chambers. Andrew Murray wrote years ago in *Abide in Christ* that if we are to be growing Christians, our "first need is to cease from striving to establish the connection with Christ more firmly, and to allow God to do it." That's the secret! I know from years of trying that growth does not occur because of my efforts. It happens when I allow God to do in and through me what I am unable to do on my own. It happens when I trust God and not myself. When I am in the process of being transformed into the likeness of Jesus, it is not *my* growth, really; it is Christ's growth *in* me.

So many of us have a spiritual history of being what one pastor, Donald McCullough, calls "huffers and puffers." We live as though our salvation depended on ourselves, not on our Savior. E. Stanley Jones wrote in *Growing Spiritually* about a woman who said, "My hands have corns on them from working and trying so hard to be good." And he responded, "She was looking at her own hands and trusting them instead of looking at the nail-pierced hands of Christ."

Oswald Chambers echoed that when he wrote, "All that we do should be founded on a perfect oneness with Him, not a self-willed determination to be godly." We need to know this, not just in our heads but deep in our bones. Without the indwelling Spirit of Jesus Christ, we cannot even take the first step down that road He asks us to travel with Him.

Yet we come so reluctantly to the place of trusting Him. In that regard we are in good company! Scripture is full of people who counted on their own efforts to make them God's people. Consider Peter who boasted he would never leave the Lord and yet, when the religious leaders turned against Jesus, Peter denied Him three times.

The words had no sooner left his lips than the rooster crowed. At that moment the Lord, being led to the dungeon of the house of the high priest, turned and looked straight at Peter. Then Peter remembered the words Jesus had spoken to him: " 'Before the rooster crows today, you will disown me three times.' And he [Peter] went outside and wept bitterly" (Luke 22:61–62).

And no wonder! On his own he couldn't even be true to his Lord. Jesus had allowed the circumstances of that night to strip Peter of the last traces of any illusion he had about his own strength. *Then* Peter was ready to love and grow and serve. But he could do this only after he was convinced of his total need of God.

Jesus tries in so many ways to tell us, as He did Peter, that we can't make it on our own. But we tend not to believe Him. We all live in the illusion that we can make it through life with just a little help from God, a little "power in a pinch." And then God kindly allows something to come along to test us. Like Peter, we fall flat on our faces and tremble in our helplessness. What a blessing, for only *then* do we begin to trust God as we should. Sometimes falling on our faces is the only way we can fall into the arms of a loving and waiting God!

DON'T QUIT—SURRENDER!

When I try to think of someone who really knows that he *can't* make it on his own, my mind goes to our friend Kent. A big, bearded hunk of a man, Kent learned to trust God the hard way, by coming to a place of desperation.

For years Kent was addicted to hard drugs. His muddled mind led him into a life of anger, violence, and bizarre activities. By the time he was 21 he had married, fathered a child, divorced, and spent numerous stints in jail. No one was able to get close to him with help. Then one night he sent a friend out with the last dollars in his pocket to get the fix he craved. As the night wore on, his friend failed to return. With morning Kent realized he was not going to come back and that he was about to go crazy—or die. Out of drugs, out of money, out of "friends," he hit bottom. It was the end.

Or was it the beginning? As a boy, Kent had gone to Sunday school. Not for long, but long enough to hear that "God is love" and that anyone who wanted help could call out to Jesus and He'd be there. Stripped of every vestige of reliance on himself, Kent had no place else to turn. So from somewhere deep inside, he cried out to God. And God answered.

Looking back to that time in his life Kent says, "It was like a miracle. God moved into my heart that morning and did *for* me what I never could have done for myself."

Now a member of both Alcoholics and Narcotics Anonymous, Kent lives his day-to-day life in Christ with the same kind of abandon and trust he demonstrated when he took that first step down the road with Him. In his wallet he carries a piece of folded paper that reads:

> Keep ever in mind the admission you made on the day of your profession in A.A. Namely that you are powerless and that it was only with your willingness to turn your life and will into My keeping that relief came to you.

Jesus' promise, "Come to Me, all who are weak and heavy laden, and I will give you rest—for My yoke is easy and My burden light" (Matthew 11:28, 30, paraphrase), is wonderfully fulfilled in Kent. He knows it is not the yoke of God, but *resistance* to the yoke that is heavy. And so Kent lives a surrendered life and carries Christ's peace wherever he goes.

I wish more of us were convinced that only as we are abandoned to Christ can we live the life for which God created us. Kent has discovered the mystery of the ages—

God's secret plan—and the sign in the back window of his pickup truck says it all:

> I didn't quit—I surrendered.

This is a lesson I have to keep learning because I have such a tendency to be a religious do-it-yourselfer. Before I was a Christian, I was certain the phrase "God helps those who help themselves" was in the Bible. It isn't. Through the years, God has allowed me to fall on my face again and again to bend me in a new direction of trust—not in myself.

Louie also struggles with this from time to time, and like me he needs to recommit himself to God's secret of growth. I remember one summer when we were driving west to do our annual family backpacking trek in the High Sierra. Our two youngest children, Jamie, who was thirteen, and Andie, who was sixteen, were with us, and Dan and Tim were going to come directly from their college campuses to meet us. Louie was unusually tired from the relentless activities of the church. As we drove, he expressed more than a few times his fatigue.

Finally Andie, a true "Jesus person," leaned over the front seat with her chin resting on her arms and began to preach to her father.

"Daddy, you get so busy and run so fast that you finally have to stop because you're exhausted. You need to learn to sit. Wait on the Lord for His strength; then you'll be able to walk and not get so weary."

Jamie made sounds of agreement. Then silence! After some time, Louie said simply, "You're right, Andie, I do need to sit. Just *sit* for a while."

After a week of camping on the shore of Lake Spotty, the children and I hiked down the mountain, leaving Louie alone with the Lord, as Andie had urged. God met Louie in those days powerfully, and Louie still alludes to that time as one of great refreshment.

SITTING IS NOT PASSIVE

I may sound as though we are to become passive people, leaving everything to God. The truth is we still must do our part. In the following chapters, we'll be looking at what our part is, but even before we begin, it is necessary to look at a paradox. We must *do* our part, yet even that doing is a *response* to His work within us. We need to understand Philippians 2:12—"Work out your salvation with fear and trembling"—in the total context of Paul's statement in the next verse: "For it is *God who works in you* to will and to act according to his good purpose."

Paul said it so clearly—and he said it again and again! "I can do everything *through him [Christ] who gives me strength*," literally, "who infuses me" with all I need (Philippians 4:13). Paul was so infused with Christ that he became a new and different person. Saul, the aggressive agitator and enemy of the faith, became Paul, the aggressive apostle and loving friend of all believers. And he always knew—and reminded others—that it was not he, but Christ *in* him who made the difference.

It is difficult to explain anything that is so mystical as the fact of Christ operating in us, as Luci Shaw tells us in her poem "Getting Inside the Miracle":

> . . . Who will diagram the gynecology
> of incarnation, the trigonometry of trinity?
> Or chemically analyze wine
> from a well? Or see inside

joints as they loosen, and whole limbs
and lives? Will anyone stand beside
the moving stone? And plot the bright
trajectory of the ascension? And explain
the tongues of fire
telling both heat and light?*

Who will map the miracle of Christ-in-us? Miracle and mystery evade our definitions—and yet we try. Dr. Paul Brand, in *Fearfully and Wonderfully Made,* likens the secret of Christ in us to the process by which DNA passes on a clear identity to each new cell: "God uses the materials and genes of natural man, splitting them apart and recombining them with his own spiritual life. . . ."

Or, from my personal life comes an image drawn from the sea. I visualize my life as a boat sitting motionless in the water, useless and still, its sails hanging limp and lifeless to the mast. Only when the unseen wind of the Spirit, God's *pneuma,* begins to fill my sails is there movement and direction. My boat has no power of its own. Only God's *pneuma* can enable it to function according to its design.

God cries out repeatedly in the Word that we can explore the very mystery of this secret plan:

"Praise be to the name of God for ever and ever; . . . He gives wisdom to the wise and knowledge to the discerning. He reveals deep and hidden things; he knows what lies in darkness, and light dwells with him.   Daniel 2:20–22

I so believe in this secret plan that it is rare for me not to begin my day with this prayer by Dr. Robert Wise:

* Reprinted from *The Secret Trees* © 1976 by Luci Shaw. Used by permission of Harold Shaw Publishers.

Jesus Christ, be in my head in my thinking,
my eyes in my seeing,
my ears in my hearing,
my mouth in my speaking,
my heart in my feeling,
my hands and feet in my doing.
I commit myself to You—body, mind, and spirit—
and ask that my life, this day, will honor You. Amen.

How can we grow into the likeness of Jesus? There is only one way: the "mystery, which is Christ in you, the hope of glory" (Colossians 1:27).

Question Ideas

1. In what ways do you still strain and strive to live your faith as though everything depended on your efforts?

2. How does this square with Christ's teaching in John 15 and Paul's continual emphasis on living *in* Christ?

3. In what ways has the secret of "Christ in you, the hope of glory" become real for you?

4. If it has not—would you be willing to make that ultimate surrender by asking Christ now to come into your life and do *for* you what you cannot do for yourself?

3

Choosing to Respond

We have seen in chapters 1 and 2 that growing into the likeness of Jesus involves a mystery. We cannot grow of our own willpower, only with His plan unfolding in us. Yet, paradoxically, we have a role to play. In this chapter we will begin exploring what our part in this process is.

It was 7 A.M. and Louie had just left the house for a breakfast meeting. Feeling a tad guilty I had decided to go for another hour's sleep. I was just making myself snug in the warmth of his side of the bed when the phone rang. Could I let it ring? No, it just might be one of the children. Padding to my study, I picked up the phone. It was Paula (not her real name).

I had met Paula recently at a dinner party. Rarely had I encountered a person so disarmingly open about her loneliness. One day she came to our house for tea. As we talked, Paula began to share deep problems. I listened for some time to this straightforward woman, compassion welling up in my heart. Finally, with uncharacteristic boldness, I said,

"Paula, I can listen to you and I can be your friend. I want to do that. But I can't solve your problems for you. You've made some bad choices and only God can give you the wisdom and the strength to turn your life around." Then I found myself asking, "Have you ever made a commitment of your life to Christ?"

"No," she answered, "but I want to do that. Right now."

Her eagerness astonished me. The two of us slipped to our knees and she whispered a short, no-nonsense prayer of acceptance of Jesus into her life. Then I prayed for her and she went on her way. It was that simple.

But it was real! Paula lost no time in joining the church, getting into a beginners' Bible study, and becoming a new disciple of Jesus Christ. In the months that followed Paula and I became real sisters. Not that we spend a lot of time with each other. But when we snatch an hour together, it is special. And always she challenges me with her probing mind and her questions.

She did on this particular morning, too, as she asked an attention-grabbing question, especially for 7 A.M.!

"Coke," she said, using my nickname, "people around the church say that we grow by allowing Jesus to live within us. Isn't there something *I* should be doing to cooperate with God? Think about it and let's have lunch." And she was gone.

Well, as usual, Paula made me think. And the pages that follow have been written partly for her, partly for me in my own quest, and for all the other Paulas who want to do their part—whatever that means—to open themselves to growth and the work of God in their lives.

WHAT ROLE DO I PLAY?

The secret of growing in His likeness is "Christ *in* us." It is God's work, not ours. But how do we open ourselves to the work of God in our lives? Surely there is something we must do!

Indeed there is! We must make choices.

That's what this chapter is all about—our choosing to

respond to God, and what that means in everyday terms.

From my own spiritual journey I have found that responding to God's work in me has required choices on my part to

1) shift the focus of my life from myself to Christ,

2) live day by day reunited with God through Christ,

3) make this relationship the highest priority of my life, and nurture the relationship by spending quality time with God.

What is quality time? For me it is time spent in worship *of* God, stillness *before* God, and communication *with* God through prayer.

To do or not to do. These are choices I must make daily, but always with the underlying awareness that the living-out of these choices is dependent on God's grace operating within my life.

Richard Foster, author and teacher, speaks to this truth by pointing out that making choices is itself an undeserved gift:

> We must ... help each other learn exactly how we are conformed to the image of Christ—and we must do that in the context of daily life. ... Our theology must confess that we are not only *saved* by grace, we *live* by it as well.

Our part then is to respond to God. Respond to the continuing work of grace by making choices that encourage God's life within us. These choices are our responsibility, within the context of grace! As Foster says, "We are not only *saved* by grace, we *live* by it as well."

RESPONSE #1: I CHOOSE TO CENTER ON CHRIST—NOT SELF

Years ago, E. Stanley Jones wrote, "The first step in growing [spiritually] is transplanting—shifting from a self-centered life to a God-centered life."

Looking at Jesus, we see that He made Himself "nothing" so that God could raise Him up (Philippians 2:7, 9). Following Jesus as our example, we are to empty ourselves of ourselves by altering the focus of our lives from *self* to *Christ*. Then, and paradoxically only then, do we find ourselves. The seed, left to itself, dies; but emptied into the earth it not only lives, but is transformed into what God created it to be. This is a promise we can count on, but it has a condition. God, the Gardener of our lives (John 15:1), wants to "transplant" us, but will not without our consent and cooperation.

Day by day and hour by hour, in ways both blatantly bold and seductively subtle, "self" battles for the front and center position in our lives. Whether we center on Christ or ourselves is *our choice*—and ours alone.

RESPONSE #2: I CHOOSE AT-ONE-MENT WITH CHRIST

If we decide in His favor, something begins to take place within us. From Genesis to Revelation, the Bible speaks of one crucial fact: We must be reunited with God. Separation kills; in union there is life. Modern psychologists agree. Noted psychiatrist Eric Fromm tells us in *The Art of Loving* that the deepest need all people have is to be rid of their sense of alienation, "to overcome separation . . . to transcend one's own individual life and find at-one-ment."

And the wonderful thing that occurs when you and I choose to respond to God's work in our lives is this: As we focus our lives on Christ and allow Him to live within us, at-one-ment begins to replace the desperate sense of loneliness and separation that has plagued humanity through the ages.

How poignantly I recall the morning after I made the decision to commit my life to Christ. I awoke to a new world, not in the sense that overnight everything had changed, but in the sense that I knew everything had *begun* to change. Jesus had entered my life and because of that gentle, strong new Presence, nothing would ever be the same for me again.

I remember trekking down the mountainside from my cabin to the dining room at Forest Home Conference Center in California. Everything seemed especially beautiful that day—the rugged mountains, the blue of the sky, the scent of the pines. Ordinary things dazzled me. I felt that I had been scrubbed on the inside, then wrapped in love. People looked different to me. But the main thing I felt was that I was no longer alone. It was my time of at-one-ment, my reuniting with God . . . I had been welcomed home.

In the fourteenth century, Julian of Norwich wrote movingly of her at-one-ment with God and referred to it repeatedly as her life's "great act of oneing"! As she put it:

> Until I am really and truly oned and fastened to God so that there is nothing created between us, I will never have full rest or complete happiness.

So being reunited, or "oned with God," as Julian winsomely described it, is crucial as we seek the answer to human separation and hope for "full rest or complete happiness." It is also crucial for all who yearn to grow in the likeness of our Lord. It is our starting place.

But once we have chosen to shift our focus from our-selves to Christ, what then? What can we do to *keep* open to God?

RESPONSE #3: I CHOOSE TO SPEND QUALITY TIME WITH GOD

Our life in Jesus is not based on legalism, but on rela-tionship. Any relationship with depth takes time. There is no way a good friendship—or a marriage with soul—will flourish without a commitment of time, where warm, open lines of communication and trust can be established. If this is true of human relationships, how much more important it is to find ways to spend quality time with our Lord.

If we spend time with God something beautiful will hap-pen. Those who immerse themselves in the Lord will begin to reflect His characteristics. They will begin to be like Him.

When Moses had his experience with God on Mt. Sinai, when he beheld the glory of the Lord, he was so completely changed that his face shone. The same can be true of us. As we spend time with God we will find our hearts changing. We may not even be aware that it is happening, but like Moses we, too, can shine as we "behold the glory of the Lord" in worship, stillness, and prayer.

BEHOLDING GOD . . .

At heart, true worship is beholding God.

And we need to have a specific time and place for this beholding worship.

When the body of believers gathers, it is a reminder to ourselves and others that God is the central focus of our lives. The time we spend together in our places of worship is meant to be "an earnest" of what we are about all the rest of the week. Worship at a special time and place helps make clear our total life commitment.

In corporate worship we behold the Lord in various ways. For instance, the music of worship can be a powerful "beholding" experience as our hearts are lifted to God through voice and instruments of praise.

I was deeply moved recently, as were other worshipers around me, when the choir of National Presbyterian Church sang "Let All Mortal Flesh Keep Silent" (Gustav Holst). There were polite sniffles—and then the sudden pulling of handkerchiefs from purse and pocket, as the Spirit of God broke into our worship in a way we had not anticipated. I wonder if choristers know what a gift they give the congregation when they lift our spirits Godward in that way?

I was equally moved in a far different setting when Louie and I were guests of our good friends Paul and Catherine Pondi in their African home village of Ngog Mapubi in Cameroon. There was that memorable drive by Jeep off the main highway halfway between Doula and the capital city of Yaounde, onto a bumpy dirt road that took us to our friends' birthplace and childhood home.

As we drew near Ngog Mapubi, smiling villagers stood on the side of the road, waving palm branches in the traditional African sign of welcome. When we arrived at the village church, hundreds of Christians were there as the local pastor and his wife gave us an official welcome—accompanied, of course, by music and that wonderful African hesitation step. What an infectious beat!

We lived in that village for four days and fell more deeply in love than ever with the African people. I stood in awe of the women—hard-working, strong, tender, and beautiful.

The sheen of their dark skin was so rich and radiant. The longer we stayed the more colorless I looked to myself. Of course, my lack of ability in French and the limits of my crash course in their Bulu language kept us from having much verbal conversation. Nevertheless, communication took place. Their eyes spoke for them and their graceful hands affirmed their nurturing capacity as they tended to our needs.

How tender was the Lord to us as we worshiped with those sisters and brothers in Christ to the beat of drums. We sang, we danced, we wept—and rarely have I experienced such pure joy in worship as I did at that time, and in that place.

. . . In the Spoken Word

Another facet of worship is "beholding God" through the spoken word. In a church, this form of worship is usually a sermon. Not that God automatically speaks through every point of every sermon, surely not that. But I do think that when one of God's servants faithfully preaches the Word of the Gospel, God honors that Word.

Before going into the pulpit to preach, Louie repeats this verse to himself: "We have this treasure in earthen vessels, to show that the transcendent power belongs to God and not to us" (2 Corinthians 4:7, RSV). Aware of his human limitations, Louie then thanks God for the privilege of being a vessel of the Word.

. . . And in the Sacraments

And in worship there is a very real "beholding" of God in the sacraments of baptism and holy Communion. Donald McCullough has so written helpfully on worship in his book

Waking from the American Dream. Speaking of the sacraments he says:

> In these little dramas symbolizing the great drama of redemption, Christ presents himself to us and confirms the reality of his gracious love.

In these "little dramas" we remember His costly death and receive His gracious love for the ongoing needs of our everyday lives. Receiving Communion is a way of responding to God's work and provision for our lives. How often, as I have eaten the bread and sipped the wine in remembrance of Him, I have walked away from the table filled with the grace I need to receive forgiveness or to give it to another, or new strength to seal a difficult decision or face up to some challenge far beyond my human capacity. At these times I am profoundly aware of God's closeness, for through the Lord's Supper my heart is touched in a very tender place.

Once, when I was hurting and much in need of this kind of closeness and grace, I slipped into a sanctuary I had never been in before. I seated myself near the rear of the church and I remember how the sun was streaming through the clear blues and reds of the stained glass windows. I recall little of the actual service until Communion was served and worshipers were invited to come to the altar to receive the bread dipped in wine from the ministering clergy. I liked that. Somehow walking down that aisle added determination to my choice to receive God's all-sufficient grace for my need. And as the young priest spoke the holy words, "My body—broken for you . . . My blood—shed for you," and placed the morsel in my mouth, I felt infused with new strength and healing for my wounds.

"The sacraments," Dale Bruner says, "are God's hugs—

they are God physically approaching and touching us." And so they were—and *are* for me.

Recently, I have discovered yet another way of seeing God in worship as I watch Susan, the interpreter in the non-hearing section of our congregation. Sunday after Sunday, Susan gives the hand signs to a small band of deaf worshipers. As I watch their response to her ministry, I see something of God in their faces that is beautiful beyond description. They obviously take delight in worship—which must please God deeply. I know it pleases me! It also convicts me as I contrast their joyous, abandoned response to God with my carefully metered out expressions of gratitude and praise.

. . . And in Quietness

Certainly one of the best ways to behold God is in the silent, still places of our hearts.

"Be still, and know that I am God" (Psalm 46:10). Through the ages saints who have heeded these words have been known as servants remarkably like their Master. Listen to what some of them have said about the importance of keeping a quiet place, just for God, in our lives.

> [Anyone] who aims at inward and spiritual things must, with Jesus, turn aside from the crowd. . . . [No one] can safely speak but he who loves silence.
>
> Thomas à Kempis

> Retire frequently with God into the inner chamber of the heart where the gentle voice of the Spirit is only heard if all be still.
>
> Andrew Murray

> Beware of the person who does not have stillness and solitude in his life. . . .
>
> Dietrich Bonhoeffer

> Spiritual growth is made or marred at the place of the devotional. . . . It is the crux. For in the devotional we expose ourselves to God's resources, we assimilate and grow by them.
>
> E. Stanley Jones

Different voices from different eras, all speaking to the same truth. There is no spiritual growth without stillness. For me, spending part of each day quietly with the Lord has become the one thing I need, above all others, to survive. Those hours are my food, my energy. Time with God is my manna, and like manna, it must be gathered every day.

In that quiet time I go most often to my special rocking chair where I read the Word, study the life of Jesus, and listen for (what Andrew Murray calls) "the gentle voice of the Spirit [which] is only heard if all be still." And sometimes I simply meditate. The Greek word for *beholding* can be translated "contemplating."

It was in Elizabeth Mulloy's wonderful little book *Your Secret Name* that I read the most helpful section on beholding. She writes:

> How do we behold? The same way Moses did: by spending time with the Lord, receiving the Word of God, and talking with God. In other words, we absorb the Lord's character by soaking up His Word (in Bible study and meditation), by talking with Him in prayer, and by learning to live in awareness of His presence. . . . [Jesus said:] "If you abide in me, and my words abide in you, ask whatever you will, and it shall be done for you" (John 15:7). He knew that if our minds are soaked, steeped in, continuously beholding His Word, then our will and our desires will be in tune with His will. Our prayers will naturally be ones that He can readily answer.

Having settled in my place, I am now ready to move toward the likeness of Jesus by praying as He prayed.

. . . And in Prayer

Clearly there is no way we can grow in the likeness of Jesus without giving time to prayer. Jesus was a Man of prayer. While He lived on earth, the connection between Himself and His Father depended on keeping that connection strong. Prayer never seemed to be a chore for Him. We can learn from Him right there: Prayer is not meant to be a grim duty, but a natural expression of dependence and affection.

Karl Barth called this need our "incurable God-sickness." Our longing for Jesus is never fully satisfied, for until we are with Him in heaven we will always want more than we have of Him here on earth.

Jesus knew that longing for His Father, so we see Him rising from bed to pray while all the world slept (Mark 1:35). Then after a draining day of ministry we see Him praying through the night (Mark 6:46). He snatched moments of stillness even as the crowds were pushing, shoving, pulling at His robe, clamoring for His help—a blind man groping his way forward, a mother cradling her sick child. Circled by all this confusion and need, Jesus sent His prayers heavenward, knowing His Father would understand His honest S.O.S. All He needed was a moment to reach out and clutch His Father's hand—and in that moment, there was strength.

Like Jesus, we should learn to snatch moments of prayer as we go through our stressful days and nights. We can *breathe* a prayer as we sit waiting in our cars at traffic lights—*beam* a prayer at children playing as we pass them on the street—*think* a prayer as we wait with an anxious neighbor in a doctor's office—*sing* a prayer as we clean a sink for the umpteenth time in one day. This kind of praying is what Brother Lawrence aptly called "practicing the presence of

God." That way we can pray at *any* time, about anything, in any place.

Jesus prayed about His life's work (Luke 3:21–23); He prayed before choosing the disciples (Luke 6:12–13); He prayed for others (Luke 22:31–32); He prayed for God to forgive others (Luke 23:34); and He prayed in the moment of death (Luke 23:46). And these are but fragments of the whole.

And so it should be for us. The disciplines of a quiet time with God spent in reflection and prayer, as well as those momentary arrow prayers, are an essential part of growing in the likeness of Jesus. Jesus taught that we "should always pray and not give up" (Luke 18:1). Indeed, all of Scripture tells us this is a necessity for spiritual health and growth. Just listen to Paul:

Pray continually.	1 Thessalonians 5:17
Be . . . faithful in prayer.	Romans 12:12
Always keep on praying.	Ephesians 6:18
Devote yourselves to prayer.	Colossians 4:2

I can almost hear someone saying, "But I don't *want* to pray. I'm not always in a praying mood." I know.

Even though quiet times have become a desperate need for me, there are times when I am not in the mood and I resist doing what I need most. At those times, the word that comes to me is *Pray anyhow*. I am sometimes rewarded with feelings of oneness with God. But there are also times when I feel absolutely nothing. And times when I *want* to pray, but I simply can't. I have no words for what I am feeling. At times of loss, the death of one loved more dearly than life itself or a wounding of spirit is so shattering and deep only God can reach its core. When life tests in this way there are no words that fit. At those times of extreme need, I believe God's hearing is particularly sharp.

Augustine said, "The best disposition for praying is that of being desolate, forsaken, stripped of everything." And the psalmist tells us that when we are *that* aware of our spiritual poverty, God hears it all—our wails, our shouts, our crying, and our "sighs too deep for words." Those too are prayers. As long as they are from our hearts, God hears and understands.

Finally, God wants us to pray (James 5:16). We pray because Jesus prayed, and we want to be like Him.

Writing on prayer, Kent and Barbara Hughes, pastor and ministry wife of The College Church in Wheaton, Illinois, put it this way in *Liberating Ministry from the Success Syndrome:*

> Our lives are like photographic plates and prayer is like a time exposure to God. As we express ourselves to God for a half hour, an hour . . . His image is imprinted more and more upon us. More and more we absorb the image of His character, His love, His wisdom, His way of dealing with life and people.

And so, we pray as a way of responding to God's work in us and as a way of keeping our hearts open to God's *continued* work in our lives. As we choose to behold Jesus in times of worship, quiet, and prayer, "His image is imprinted more and more upon us." The miracle of growing into the likeness of our Master is taking place!

Question Ideas

1. In what way is corporate worship a nurturing part of your life? (Or do you perhaps sit in worship and think about what you will fix for lunch?)

2. How might private worship become more meaningful to you? Do you truly believe that spending quality time with God will imprint His image on your life?

3. When did you last spend a time of quiet before the Lord, expecting Him to meet you in a special way?

4. If you believe that by giving God quality time the image of Jesus will be "imprinted more and more upon you," how do you plan to respond in terms of your priorities?

4
The Word As an Agent of Growth

An eager new believer stood up at a seminar on spiritual growth and asked, "What are the three most important steps that I as a new Christian should take to begin to grow?"

Without a moment's hesitation, the woman at the podium responded, "First, study the Scriptures, then apply them to life. Second, study the Scriptures, then apply them to life. Third, study the Scriptures, then apply them to life."

Jesus points us in that same direction. He was a Man of the Word. His life demonstrated that at every turn. As He grew, Scripture was at the core of His learning. By the time He was twelve years old, He was able to interpret and expound upon the Scriptures in a way that astounded the rabbis in the Temple (Luke 2:46–47)! In His first sermon, He reached back to Isaiah 61 and claimed it for Himself:

> "The Spirit of the Lord is on me, because he has anointed me to preach good news to the poor. He has sent me to proclaim freedom for the prisoners and recovery of sight for the blind, to release the oppressed, to proclaim the year of the Lord's favor."
>
> Luke 4:18–19

In Jesus' struggle in the wilderness, Satan tried to tempt Him, but Jesus used Scripture to resist the attacks. The Word was for Him both a shield and a sword.

Throughout His ministry people were amazed by His fresh insights and undisputed authority when He taught the Scriptures. Jesus took Scripture to new levels of meaning (Matthew 7) and was Himself the capstone of revelation.

Finally, in death, He spoke Scripture from the cross as He agonized, "My God, my God, why have you forsaken me?" (Psalm 22:1, Mark 15:33).

In every way Jesus was a Man of the Word. He studied it and lived it. If you and I are to grow into His likeness, we too must study the Scriptures and apply them to our lives in the way Jesus did.

In his book *Growing Spiritually,* E. Stanley Jones talks about creating the right conditions for growth. We are most spiritually receptive, he says, when we are studying the Scriptures in meditation. "Then," he says, "the pores of our being are open to God and life, and we are receptive to our fingertips."

GOD'S WORD: SHARP, DISCERNING, MIRROR-LIKE

How true! When God speaks to us through the Bible something happens. Unlike the words of our most trusted human friends, God's Word is swift and active and never misses the target. It moves smartly to the core of every life situation. Hebrews 4:12–13 describes Scripture as

> . . . living and active.   Sharper than any doubled-edged sword, it penetrates even to dividing soul and spirit, joints and marrow; it judges the thoughts and attitudes of the heart.

Indeed, for me the Bible is a mirror in which I see how far I have to go even to resemble remotely the Lord I love.

Again and again, the light of Scripture reveals the inconsistency and impurity of my heart.

Recently, for instance, I was restless in my spirit because of someone who, in my opinion, was unfairly critical of a ministry in which I believe and am personally involved. I know this ministry to be valid. Hurt and angry, I went to a time of quiet with the Lord, feeling indignant. "Do something, Lord! Vindicate Your work and Your servants!"

But the word God gave me that day, as a plumb line by which my attitude had to be measured, was this:

> "If someone strikes you on the right cheek, turn to him the other also. . . . You have heard that it was said, 'Love your neighbor and hate your enemy.' But I tell you: Love your enemies and pray for those who persecute you."   Matthew 6:39, 43–44

Ouch! God was going to "do something" all right . . . in *me!* I haven't found a way yet to serve this woman, but I am building a relationship with her and I trust that out of the relationship a way will come. It isn't easy; Scripture is tough! As Paul Tournier says, "In the Bible, God does not take people out of his drama; but he lives it with them and for them. The Bible avoids nothing. It enters realistically into our life as it is."

Yes, the Bible is a mirror for our lives—and it is more.

SCRIPTURE LEADS TO CLEANSING

In John 15:3 Jesus says to His friends: "You are already clean because of the word I have spoken to you." For people of the Word, Scripture is a powerful agent of God's cleansing—and thus makes spiritual growth possible.

The Word is an agent of authenticity. Human wisdom is not. Knowledge by itself yields absolutely zero spiritual growth. Indeed, it could make us dangerous people, "having a form of godliness but denying its power" (2 Timothy 3:5). Our study of Scripture should never be to gain knowledge in and of itself, but to change the way we think and live.

In *Abide in Christ* Andrew Murray put it this way: "Keep the commandments in the love of your heart. Be not content to have them in the Bible for reference, but have them transferred by careful study, by meditation and by prayer, by a loving acceptance, by the Spirit's teaching, to the fleshly tables of the heart."

For me, this means focusing on a specific passage of Scripture and lingering there long enough for it to make its transforming mark on my life.

I remember years ago, as a brand-new convert, I went to Jesus and asked Him where I should begin. I had not only a new way of life to learn, but old ways to unlearn. My sense was that God knew far better than I where I needed to start. And indeed He did!

Not surprisingly, I began by reading and rereading the Gospels. I spent more than a year "living" in the Beatitudes of Jesus. I studied them in different translations, read commentaries about them, meditated on them, prayed over them, but above all I asked God to make them part of me. I came to think of the Beatitudes as the "attitudes that ought to be." They became the plumb line against which all my attitudes in the years that followed were to be measured. I lingered long in Matthew 5 and still return to it often. When we "soak" in the truth of God as we find it in Scripture and then, by God's grace, begin applying this truth to our lives, it is a powerful agent of change.

"Study the Scriptures. ['Marinate' in them until they are part of you.] Then apply them to daily life!"

SCRIPTURE IS PERSONAL

Scripture is a feast God has provided for us. There is help in the Bible for each life situation you and I will ever face.

A friend once had a dream in which she found herself in a large room with only one door. There were other people in the room, too, all of them distraught, many of them weeping.

Then the door opened and Jesus entered the room. To the man nearest Him He said, "Why are you crying?"

"O Lord," the man said, "I cry because I never became the person I wanted to be. I was always so busy trying to get ahead, so worried about making ends meet. I always meant to do it, but the truth is, I never found time for You."

"Then you didn't get My letter?"

"What? Lord, You wrote me a letter?"

"Oh, yes. I said, 'Consider the lilies of the field, how they grow. They toil not, neither do they spin. If that is how I clothe the grass of the field . . . will I not much more clothe you? So do not worry . . . but seek first My Kingdom, and what you need for life will be provided.' "

"Lord!" the man cried. "I've heard that, of course, but I didn't know it was for me!"

"But it was, it was," Jesus said with sadness, and moved on to the next person.

"And you, My child, why are you sad?"

The woman replied, "Lord, my husband was taken so

long ago and I never got over his death. I was young and my life has been so lonely. You know, Lord, I have ached for companionship."

Again He said, "And you didn't get My letter?"

"No, Lord. A letter? I didn't know. . . ."

"Yes, and in the letter I told you, 'Blessed are those who mourn, for they will be given courage and comfort,' and I promised to be with you always, even to the very end. I said I would never leave you."

"Oh, yes, I remember now. The minister read those words at my husband's funeral and they were written on cards friends sent me, but I thought they were just . . . well, words. I had no idea You meant them for me!"

And on around the room He went, speaking to everyone there. When He had finished, each person had learned something that kept him or her from living with holy abandon. There had been big obstacles and little ones blurring their spiritual awareness. Every person had received a personalized word, an individual correction, counsel, guidance, a promise of provision, companionship, forgiveness, healing, comfort, and love. Everything needed for healing, fullness of life, and service.

Yet no one realized the Word of God was meant for him or for her.

"Colleen, do you know God has written letters to you?" my friend asked after she told me about her dream.

I considered my answer carefully. "Yes, I believe God has spoken, and continues to speak, to me. But," I had to add, "I do not believe it enough."

Then I remembered Henrietta Mears, that amazing teacher who encouraged and inspired me during my early days as a Christian. Miss Mears trusted God, it seemed to me, with every fiber of her being. And yet shortly before her death she was asked, "If you had your life to live over, would you do anything differently?"

Without needing to reflect more than a few seconds, she answered, "Yes, I would believe God more."

God, help me, for I too would believe You more as You speak to me through Your Word.

GOD SPEAKS THROUGH OTHER BOOKS, TOO

God also speaks through the words of others as recorded in wonderful books that have come into my life. These writers pass on Christ's truth through the filter of their own experiences.

Oswald Chambers, Thomas Merton, Andrew Murray, E. Stanley Jones, Amy Carmichael, James S. Stewart, Julian of Norwich, Thomas à Kempis, Elizabeth O'Connor, Henri Nouwen, John Bunyan . . . have all become my spiritual companions. They consistently speak to my needs. And there are others. The prayers of Baillie, Raines, and Quoist relay yearnings of my heart in ways I feel but am not always able to express. And there are the classic prayers I rediscover, as though for the first time, in *The Book of Common Prayer*.

I am deeply grateful to these people and others—from past and present—who never fail to provide a word from God that nourishes my spirit.

GOD'S FIRST AND LAST WORD: CHRIST, THE LIVING WORD

But there is one voice above every other that I need to hear. More than 500 years ago, Thomas à Kempis put it so well:

> With the Prophet Samuel, I humbly and earnestly entreat: Speak, Lord, for Thy servant heareth. Speak, O Lord God, Inspirer and Enlightener of all the Prophets; for they, without Thee, will avail me nothing. They may indeed sound forth words, but they give not the spirit. Most beautifully do they speak; but if Thou be silent, they inflame not the heart. They give the letter, but Thou disclosest the sense. They publish the mysteries, but Thou unlockest the meaning of the things signified. They declare the commandments, but Thou enablest us to fulfill them. They show the way, but Thou givest strength to walk in it. What they can do is only from without, but Thou instructest and enlightenest the heart. . . . Speak then, O Lord, for Thy servant heareth; for Thou hast the words of eternal life.

Growing in the likeness of Jesus means becoming *people of the Word*. It means "studying the Scriptures and applying them to life." It means allowing Scripture to be the powerful agent of change and growth God means it to be. But above all else, it means knowing the Living Word who dwells within our hearts. It is the Living Word within us who transforms us from the inside out— Christ, the Living Word, who nourishes and feeds us, enabling us to move toward our goal of growing in His likeness.

Question Ideas

1. In what way does the Word of God affect change in your life? Would you be willing to increase the role Scripture plays in your life?

2. How does the Word speak most powerfully to you? In convicting? Correcting? Comforting? Guiding?

3. How has "soaking" in the Scriptures helped you grow in the likeness of Jesus?

5

As We Trust We Grow

So far, as we have been exploring the art of growing into the likeness of Jesus, we have seen that spending time with Him is the secret; He does the transforming.

And we have been looking at ways of spending time with Jesus. We find Him in worship. We find Him in the Word. And in this chapter we will see how we also find Him in an *attitude*—the heart's attitude of trust.

At some point, as we spend quality time with Jesus, we will hear the words *Follow Me*.

I have often wondered if Jesus meant these words as a command or an invitation.

I'm not sure.

What I do know from the Bible is that once the call was made and a man or woman responded positively, that person was never the same again.

And it is no less true for people today. When Jesus approaches our lives and we say *yes,* everything begins to be different for us as well.

As I was studying this "follow Me" passage in Matthew, I asked Louie for some help with the Greek. With his expertise I discovered some interesting things about the word *follow*. It was frequently used of soldiers and slaves, for instance. In the Gospels, it is rooted in the Greek word for *road*. So when Jesus says, "Follow Me," He is using a term often used by people in command, and He is asking us to walk down the same road with Him.

But there is more. The Greek word also carries the idea of being *like* the one we follow. Having what we think and do be in conformity with the person who leads us. How well that squares with my "ah ha" verse in Matthew 10: *"It is enough for the servant to be like his master."*

For that says to me it is not enough simply to walk down the same road with Jesus, enjoying His company. Nor is it enough to be involved in religious activities and to follow His ethical example. It is not enough until we are literally *growing in His likeness,* being consistent with and conformed to the image of the One we follow (2 Corinthians 3:16–18)!

I'm thinking of a man I stood behind in a checkin line at the airport not too long ago. Someone had fouled up his seating assignment, and he was furious. He stood there bellowing at the stunned airline employee, making demeaning remarks that she took most graciously.

Finally, with boarding pass in hand, he stomped off toward the gate in a rage. At that point, the patient airline agent was close to tears but she said simply to all of us within earshot, "What a grouch!" We agreed with her and gave her some affirmation for keeping her cool. But I was on my way to a very special gathering of Christians in a faraway city so, as I anticipated that pleasant event, I soon forgot the disagreeable traveler and the unpleasant episode.

That night I went to the opening session of my conference and I could not believe my eyes. There he was, none other than the "grouch" himself! Only now he wore a big smile as he stood on the platform leading that assembly in worship and praise.

I confess I had trouble that night responding to his leadership. I couldn't help picturing him standing before the airline employee and attacking her. But the point I want to stress here is that at *that* moment he was not being consistent with and conformed to the One he claimed to follow.

We all stumble and fall, make mistakes and disappoint people. But as we seek to grow in the likeness of Jesus, we should hope to have fewer and fewer of those inconsistent episodes.

Perhaps the times we catch ourselves blaming others are good times to reevaluate our desire to be like Jesus.

Andrew Murray expressed it this way: "The holy life of Jesus, with His feelings and disposition, is breathed into us by the Holy Spirit. The believers' calling is to think and feel and will just what Jesus thought and felt and willed."

As I think of Jesus I am persuaded that His absolute trust in His Father was the basis for all that He did. Hebrews 11:6 tells us "without faith it is impossible to please God" and faith, simply put, is trust. Jesus pleased God well (Matthew 3:16–17) because He trusted, was obedient to, and came to speak and act on God's behalf. Jesus depended on His Father for *everything* (John 12:44–50) and this is what we are meant to do as we follow after Christ.

Here we have an essential step if we are to grow into the likeness of Jesus. *Trust* is the *sine qua non* of the spiritual life. We are to put our trust in God—*not* ourselves. Without this basic trust it will be impossible for us to please God.

Our daughter, Andie, has recently given birth to a third child, a beautiful baby girl. I love going to Andie's home, ostensibly to lend a helping hand, but I suspect I really go to bask in the joy of their company. I especially enjoy watching Lara, the baby, while Andie is nursing her, witnessing a holy bonding taking place between them.

Little Lara watches her mother's face intently, and when their eyes meet she grins so widely the milk trickles out the corners of her mouth. My memory takes me back a generation and I see four other tiny faces looking into my eyes with the same abandon and trust. Emotion grabs at my throat and fills my eyes. My daughter speaks, and I am unable to answer her. It is a tender moment, and we both understand.

Later Lara's father comes home. Craig greets six-year-old Caitlin with a hug, searches for four-year-old Peter who is playing hide-and-seek with him, and then reaches for the baby. Lifting Lara, Craig gently balances her in the air above him. She gurgles happily, certain that her father will do her no harm.

I am struck by her lack of fear, just as I was with our own children when Louie, at another time and place, tossed them about. Lara trusts Andie and Craig for everything.

In much the same way, we are meant to trust God: simply, with abandon, for everything, even—no, especially when the going is tough! As Ben Patterson says in his splendid book *Waiting,* "All we can cling to is that even though we do not know *why* God does what He does, we can know that nothing thwarts His purpose, and that in all things He works for our good." God wills the best for us and will never let us go. . . . *That,* we can trust!

That is our goal, to trust without reservation, as a child trusts good and loving parents. And as Jesus trusted His Father. But that is not easy. Our old nature wants to be in charge because our natural desire for control and autonomy dies hard. As I think about this tendency within all of us, I decide it must run in the family. Adam and Eve, our first human parents, had a deadly desire to seize control of their own lives. "You can snatch God's power," Satan taunted, and they believed his lie.

How different that desire is from growing into the likeness of Jesus! For when we become more like Him, rather than *seeking God's place,* we are learning to *allow* God that rightful place above every other. We desire the will of God more than anything in the world and are ready to lay aside our own plans for God's. It means we give up our self-centered attempts to run our own lives and give over control to God. William Barclay said: "God's wisdom knows what is best for us, God's love desires what is best for us, God's power can bring about what is best for us."

Wouldn't we be foolish not to love and trust a God like that? And this kind of childlike trust should ultimately lead us to . . .

THE NATURAL OUTCOME OF TRUSTING: OBEDIENCE

Jesus not only *trusted* the Father, He was *obedient* in every way (Hebrews 5:8, Matthew 26:42). The old Gospel hymn had it right, "For there's no other way . . . But to trust and obey," and it had the order right, too! For trust is a prerequisite for obedience. Like two beats of a heart, both are necessary if our faith is to grow. Jesus linked obedience and discipleship forever when He said, "You are My friends *if* you do what I command" (John 15:14).

But if we have a struggle learning to trust God, we have a battle royal when it comes to obedience. I believe the single most difficult thing most of us must relinquish as we follow Jesus is our own autonomy. Like Adam and Eve, the desire to control our own lives has a deadly grip on us!

Louie and I know about that "grip" from painful experience. Early in our marriage, while still in seminary, we shared a deep longing to serve Christ in Africa. We have always had a special interest in Africa and her people. We took that desire of our hearts as indication of a call from God. During our years at San Francisco Theological Seminary in San Anselmo, California, and two years of postgraduate work in Scotland, we prepared for what we believed was to be our life's call. We read, studied, attended mission conferences, sought out students from Africa. We packed the wedding gifts we thought inappropriate or impractical for our calling to a foreign culture into barrels to give away. We even planned our children close in age (four in five years!) so they could be playmates for one another if we were sent to an isolated field. We could scarcely wait to begin.

When Louie completed his postgraduate work, we got bookings on a freighter, returned to the United States from Scotland, and went immediately to the Presbyterian Board of Missions in New York. Eagerly we presented ourselves and our "perfect plan" . . . perfect, except for one major flaw. It was *ours* and not God's. Our mission board had no place for us that year. A doctor, a nurse, those they could use, but not a preacher-teacher with a pregnant wife.

We were devastated. What had gone wrong? We were so willing, so ready to go. Never mind that it was to a place of our own choosing . . . how could anything that seemed so right be wrong?

In time we began to realize the desperate hold our own desires had on us. It was a humbling time. More than a moment of truth, it was months of wondering and waiting and not knowing anything certain about our future. Then slowly we began to understand that obedience is to follow Jesus down *His* road and disobedience is insisting on taking the road of our own choosing. It was difficult for us to let go of our dream, but it was an absolutely necessary and basic lesson we had to learn. God was in charge, we were not! This was the beginning of our conviction that we are not to control our own destinies. We are people under orders!

Looking back over the years, I am so grateful this is so. Now I cannot imagine wanting to take that ultimate responsibility again for my life—or the life of anyone I love—when our wise, loving, and powerful Lord is willing to assume it for me.

And how lovingly God has led us through our ministry, often putting us into situations we would never have chosen, but places that were unmistakably right. Perhaps not for "our advancement," but for the Kingdom of God. And that, after all, is what life is all about for the disciple, isn't it?

FOLLOWING JESUS INTO THE UNKNOWN

Paul spoke of the "obedience that comes from faith" (Romans 1:5, 16:26). When we trust God, we will *want* to be obedient. We may not understand why we are led down a certain road, nor will we know what waits for us around the next bend. Often the following will not be easy. Life will test us and at times obedience is learned in the arena of pain. But if it were always easy, there would be no need to trust.

And remember, in the life Jesus lived on earth He too had to learn obedience and it wasn't any easier for Him than it is for us. In fact, His obedience took Him down a road that led to a Roman cross. The same temptations we face, and more, came to Him (Hebrews 4:15), and to say no to them, He had to fast and pray and continually remind Himself He was not here to fulfill His own plans for His life. He was under orders from His Father.

So there is no question about it! If you and I want to grow

in the likeness of Jesus we must walk by faith down the road of trust and obedience. Trusting hearts create obedient wills and they will go down any road where they hear their Lord calling, "Follow Me."

Question Ideas

1. As you grow older are you more dependent on material things for security and identity?

2. What things or what people in your life do you tend to trust more than God?

3. In what way is trust related to the anxiety level in your life?

4. If you say you trust but are not willing to *obey* God, what does that say about your relationship?

6

Growing Like Him Through Acts of Love

We find Jesus in worship. We find Him in the Word. And we draw closer to Him through an attitude of the heart—trust. Through all of these ways He performs His transforming work in our lives.

He also is found in acts of love.

"Of all the worn, smudged, dog-eared words in our vocabulary, 'love' is surely the grubbiest, smelliest, slimiest. Bawled from a million pulpits, it has become an outrage to good taste and decent feeling, an obscenity which one hesitates to pronounce. And yet it has to be pronounced, for, after all, *love is the last word.*"

These words of Aldous Huxley make a point. *Love* is surely the most used, overused, and misused word in our language.

The Roman world into which Jesus was born must have abused their words for *love* in the same way, for the early disciples did not want the love they experienced in Jesus Christ to be confused with any previous notions. So they coined a new word—*agape*—taken from the commonly used verb *agapao.*

AGAPE, A UNIQUE SIGN

Agape signaled: "This love is unique; it can be known only in God through the Person of Jesus Christ."And it is in *this* love that we find Jesus.

The apostle John said, "God is love" (1 John 4:16). John was not telling us that along with other wonderful attributes God *has* love; rather, He *is* love. This is the essence, the core of God's character. In his Gospel, John emphasized the crucial nature of love as he quoted Jesus: "My command is this: Love each other as I have loved you" (John 15:12). "All men will know that you are my disciples if you love one another" (John 13:35). Love, Jesus said, was the one convincing verification of discipleship. Therefore, walking down the same road with Jesus will mean that we must learn to walk with love in our hearts. By this sign, people will know that we have chosen His road and that we belong to Him.

In *Abide in Christ* Andrew Murray wrote that for Christians a "life of love is the chief evidence of their faith, their proof to the world that God sent Christ, and that He has shed abroad in them the same love with which He loved Him. Of all the evidence of Christianity, this is the mightiest and most convincing."

So all of us who want to grow in the likeness of Jesus by spending time with Him, will find Him in love.

But not just *any* kind of love. Our great need is not for sentiment; it is for *agape*, that unique quality of unconditional caring the early disciples saw only in their Lord.

AGAPE REFLECTS GOD'S LOVE

But what *was* it that made it so unusual, so different from any other notion of love, that the early Christians gave it a name all its own? Let's look again at the words of Jesus:

"As the Father has loved me, so have I loved you."

John 15:9

We can begin to understand the nature of *agape* as we see how the Father loves Jesus, the Son. Scripture paints a picture for us of parental delight and pleasure: "This is my Son, whom I love; with him I am well pleased" (Matthew 3:17).

Scripture also paints the Father's love as overflowing: "The Father loves the Son and has placed everything in his hands" (John 3:35). God's love for the Son passes understanding. And yet, with all its delight, its generosity, its surpassing power, Andrew Murray points out an incredible fact: "This love of God to the Son must serve . . . as the glass in which you are to learn how Jesus loves you."

Can it be true? Does Jesus really love us as much as God the Father loves Him?

I find it difficult to believe, but I know Christ speaks truth, and just because truth is beyond my comprehension does not mean it is not real. If Jesus said it, it is true, and that means we are to Him more important and more precious than we can ever know. Our lives are bound together. Christ longs for us to be one with Him.

AGAPE MIRRORS THE WAY WE ARE TO LOVE

This is indeed love and grace beyond our understanding, yet we are to believe it.

But not love to keep selfishly to ourselves. Jesus made that very clear when He went on to say, "My command is this, love one another in the same way." Jesus calls it a "new" commandment, which seems strange when, from the very beginning, God has said we were to love our neighbors as ourselves.

But loving as Christ loved *was* new. His kind of caring lifted love a giant step above any conceivable human expression into a new place beyond knowledge, understanding, and common sense. For Jesus loved His disciples then, and He loves us now, *totally,* without equivocation and without our doing anything to deserve such love.

Brennan Manning writes: "[God loves] beyond fidelity and infidelity, beyond worthiness and unworthiness—without caution, without limit, without boundary or breaking point." And that is not the way we humans, left on our own, deal with one another.

Oh, we may manage fairly well when it comes to loving family and friends, people who are good to us and who love us in return. But let someone treat us unfairly or become less than complimentary, and we tend to bristle, to become defensive and hostile. If not outwardly, then in our hearts. I know I do. Then I remember Jesus and my longing to become more like Him. I see Him moving through the Gospels with love at the core of all His relationships, even the difficult ones. Especially those!

AGAPE IS MEANT FOR ENEMIES

And then I think of His relationship with Judas. Perhaps because of my interest in theater, I visualize the scene. I picture the disciples in the Upper Room having supper together on that last Passover night. . . . I see Jesus rising, mid-meal, to act out a parable as an example of the way He meant His followers to serve one another. Girding Himself with a towel, He picks up a basin of water and moves from disciple to disciple, performing the task of the most humble household servant, a task reserved only for non-Jewish slaves.

Then He comes to Judas, knowing precisely what he is about to do. And without a moment's hesitation, Jesus kneels before Judas, too, washing His betrayer's feet. As I envision this amazing scene, I believe there *has* to be a moment when their eyes meet, and with a look that must pierce the heart, Jesus lets Judas know there is *nothing* he can do that will *ever* make Him stop loving him. . . .

But it had to hurt deeply, for these two had been brothers. Aren't wounds caused by those we love the ones that cause the most pain? Jesus must have ached inside when, at the moment of the betrayal, Judas called Him "friend." And yet Jesus forgave him. His love didn't stop.

Such love astonishes me—particularly when I think of the betrayals I have known (every life has a Judas or two in it) and recall how difficult it has been for me to love the persons involved. My natural tendency has been to clutch my hurt with one hand and hold my betrayer at arm's length with the other, making sure that person never gets near enough to strike again. But Jesus has a better way and I want to learn from Him. He becomes a servant to the very one who would do Him in. No distancing, no protecting of self. Rather than pull away, He draws close, close enough to wash feet and look into eyes, close enough to keep loving, to forgive, and, yes, to take the risk of being wounded and scarred . . . again!

ANSWERS SELDOM COMFORT, BUT AGAPE DOES

Some years ago I had to take that risk with my father, who had disappeared from my life when I was a baby. Then, quite out of the blue, my father called me one night on the telephone and wanted to come back into my life. As a small child I had ached to know him, but now, thirty-plus years later, I had a husband and four children of my own and I was not at all sure I cared to open that old wound. He had, after all, betrayed my mother, the most wonderful woman in the world to me. Why, after a lifetime of silence, broken by only two brief meetings, did he want to know me now?

I wrestled with that question until God, and Louie, got through to me. Their message was simple and clear. I *had* to forgive him for all the past hurts, to love him and be willing to be a partner in building a relationship that would start from well behind the normal starting line.

I want you to know that from a human point of view I had neither the desire nor the love I needed to move in that direction. Yet when I confessed this and asked for the resources of Christ's *agape,* I was given both. I remember our first real evening together as though it were yesterday.

As Louie and I drove to San Diego's Town and Country Inn to meet my father and his wife, Lucille, I rehearsed the questions I felt I had a right to ask. Real guilt-triggers like, "Where have you been all the years I really needed you?"

But when we were actually together—the four of us seated at a small table in the dining room of the Inn—a small miracle occurred. My desire to tell my father how much he had hurt me simply disappeared. Instead I sat, silent for the most part, watching this man who was somehow a part of me. His eyes were a remarkable blue, and when he turned to speak to Louie, giving me a full profile, I thought: "Ah ha, so that's where my nose comes from!"

At the end of the evening I realized, here was a man who'd had deep needs in his own life. I didn't have to have answers. Besides, I have discovered over the years that answers seldom comfort: God does! Christ *in* me would enable me to forgive and to enter into a relationship with him and his lovely wife. And He did!

In fact, He even showed me simple ways in the next two years, which were my father's last, in which I could wash his feet . . . and he could wash mine. I wouldn't have missed that for anything, although without the presence of Jesus' *agape* it would have been impossible.

At the close of *The Bridge of San Luis Rey,* Thornton Wilder wrote, "All impulses of love return to the love that made them. Even memory is not necessary for love. There is a land of the living and a land of the dead, and the bridge to love the only survival, the only meaning."

I was glad for the bridge of love that made a way for a father and daughter to touch while there was still time. And I was deeply grateful to his Lucille, who is a fine woman in every way, and who I am sure was responsible for my father's call that moved us toward each other.

Admittedly, it isn't easy to yield to God's way when we feel we are justified in our anger and hurt. But what a price we pay when we refuse the gift of grace and are not willing to allow God to do *in* us what we cannot do for ourselves.

AGAPE HAS COSTLY ALTERNATIVES

When we refuse to move toward Jesus' likeness in the ways of love, there are some costly alternatives. We become troubled, guilt-ridden people. Failure to love creates the heaviest burden in the world. It weighs us down, exhausts us, decreases our effectiveness in our work . . . yet we stubbornly resist God's way. We are what the poet e. e. cummings calls "un-dead" people—unable to respond to life and to those who need us.

And that isn't all. When we won't love ourselves—or others—with God's unique *agape*, we become bitter and cynical, cut off from ourselves, others, and God. The resulting isolation strains friendships and tears families apart. Some people turn to drugs or to compulsive sex because they can't stand the loneliness. Others develop an appetite for failure. But all punish themselves in some way. Our hospitals, institutions, and even our churches are full of people who are not willing to love.

But why? Why do we cling to misery, hug our burdens, and refuse to let go of a lifetime of "junk"? Why do we so often refuse to go God's way?

I'm convinced that most people, certainly most of us who call ourselves Christians, yearn as I do to be free of all the extra baggage that weighs us down. As Jesus' servants, we *want* to love the way He does. We simply don't think it is realistic. Someplace along the way we bought into the rationale so common today that to love in the way He does is not possible for earthlings like us. So we live our earthbound, half-conscious lives. And all the while God has made it so clear: There is a better way for us. God sent Jesus to show us that way, and gave us the Word to command us to "love as He loves." And there are so many facets to God's love. We will never be able to fathom its reach and depth. Like a diamond in the sun, it explodes in every direction and beyond our sight, with beauty and light.

AGAPE IS UNCONDITIONAL

For example, unlike ours, God's love does not lay conditions or expectations on us. God has high dreams for our lives, but God's love does not depend on our fulfilling those dreams. If we do not perform, love is not withdrawn.

I have a dear friend who tends to be a perfectionist. She is very duty- and task-oriented, generous with others, but hard on herself. Dee says her life changed when she heard and believed these words: "There is nothing you can do that will ever make God stop loving you and nothing you can do to make God love you more."

That freed her and it can free us, too. God loves us. Period. That is God's nature and even our purest human love does not prepare us to understand that truth. I am reminded of Isaiah 49:15, paraphrased here:

> "Can a mother forget her baby? Be without tenderness for the child of her womb? Even if she *should* forget—I will never forget you."

AGAPE IS FOREVER

And that brings us to another facet of God's love: It lasts forever! "I have loved you with an everlasting love" (Jeremiah 31:3). In eternity Christ loved and longed for those who had been given Him by God. Andrew Murray said: "And when He came and told His disciples that He loved them, it was indeed not with a love of earth and of time, but with the love of eternity. And it is with that same infinite love that His eye still rests upon each of us."

Imagine! This forgiving, sacrificial, tender, unconditional love Jesus has for us has always been and will always be. There is nothing tentative, conditional, or temporary about it. And, impossible as it may seem, we are commanded to love one another in the same way.

I can almost hear you say, "Love like Jesus? How can that be?"

I know.

I ask the same question.

It seems so presumptuous until I remember that it is God's idea—not mine—and it was not a nice suggestion, it was a command. And, in the words of Mother Teresa, "Our great God would never command the impossible."

So, *how* can it be?

For me the answer is found in Scripture in a progression of events that is crucial to loving as Jesus loves.

THREE STEPS TOWARD AGAPE

1. "Love because he first loved us" (1 John 4:19). I must believe God's amazing love for me. I must know, bone-deep, that I am loved by God before I will be able to love others with abandon. For only by allowing Christ's powerful love to burn like sunlight through the smoggy haze of my doubts and insecurities am I able to take that risk. Remember the song Bill and Gloria Gaither wrote together? "I am loved, I am loved—I can risk loving you." That's it!

God's love gives me value not because of what I do or

achieve, but because the Lord of all life has accepted me and declared me worthy. From this base I am able to give myself, in love, to others. But only then.

When you and I become vessels of Christ's love we also receive beyond measure. Paradoxically, giving love reinforces a godly and healthy self-esteem that enables us to care for ourselves. As the receiver is blessed, so is the giver—by the very act of love itself.

2. Abide in Christ's love. In John 15 Jesus linked abiding to His command to love as He loved. "Abide in my love . . . love one another, as I have loved you" (verses 10, 12, KJV).

When we abide in Jesus, and in His love, we are in a love that passes knowledge. As we receive all of love's fullness, we learn to love. With Christ abiding in us, the Holy Spirit pours the love of God into our hearts. Then we can love the most difficult and unlovable people with a love that is not our own, but that of Jesus in us.

3. Allow Christ to love through you. Love is never to be a work we perform. Rather, in the words of Andrew Murray, it is the "result of the spontaneous outflowing of a life from within, and the mighty in-working of love from above." Jesus said, "Abide in me, and I in you. As the branch cannot bear fruit of itself except it abide in the vine; no more can ye, except ye abide in me. . . . Continue ye in my love" (John 15:4, 9, KJV).

For me, this has become the secret of living as Jesus commands. It is impossible, absolutely impossible, if we are trusting ourselves, depending on our own strength, our own efforts to make us into something we are not. Our own resources will never be enough to help us love in a way that resembles His likeness. But it is *not* impossible if we are trusting Christ to do *in* us and *for* us what we could never do for ourselves.

I have tried it both ways. Straining and striving in love's direction on my own power, I have failed utterly. My love goes just so far—and that is not enough. Only when I admit I am helpless to love as He loves, and allow Him to do it for me, am I able to obey His command. I will do the reaching out to people, but the love must come from Him.

So I am no longer asking God to give me *more* love— "Please a little here, Lord, and a bit more there where mine is wearing thin"—as though love were some kind of commodity. Rather, I am learning to pray:

"Lord, let me live this day yielded to You. And let love be the natural manifestation of Your life within me."

His life within provides the love I long to have for others. Temple Gardner of Cairo used to say, "Not I, but Christ loving through me." In Him we have it all. It is His work and His power and we have the privilege of being His vessels. "We have this treasure in earthen vessels, that the excellency of the power may be of God, and not of us" (2 Corinthians 4:7, KJV).

Yes, it is possible really to love as Jesus did. Even the thought is so high we can hardly take it in. Yet there it is: Jesus, dreaming for us, working for us, offering us everything we need to make His command come true. Now it is up to us.

Will we believe His love for us?

Will we abide in His love?

Will we yield our lives to Him each day so that love becomes the natural manifestation of Christ in us?

Will we?

The living out of Jesus' command to love one another—as He loves us—and thereby grow in His likeness depends on our response.

The choice is always ours.

Question Ideas

1. Jesus says in John 15:12, "My command is this: Love each other as I have loved you." Does this command seem an impossibility to you? If so, explain.

2. Would God command the impossible?

3. In what way is the idea of Christ loving through you a new thought?

4. Have you had the experience of God's using you to love someone difficult? Would you be willing to share such an experience with others?

5. Forgiveness is inherent in love. Would you mind sharing your greatest challenge in forgiving someone? How did Christ make that possible for you?

7

Beholding Jesus in Our Thoughts

Perhaps the most difficult of all places to find Jesus is in our thoughts. We can make an effort to be a person of the Word; we can learn to trust Him more every day; we can be vessels of His *agape*.

But to find Him in our thoughts . . . that's hard. Our thoughts are secret. They are the result of lifetimes of conditioning. They seem to have lives of their own, springing unbidden into our minds, refusing to obey our commands to take this direction or that.

Perhaps because of this Jesus made a point of stressing a brand-new way of thinking. When He approached Peter, Andrew, James, and John and asked them to drop what they were doing, He was telling them literally to leave everything, to walk with Him in a totally new direction.

Including the very way they thought.

In Matthew 5 He spells out what that means. Six times in the last half of that chapter Jesus says, "You have heard it said . . . but I say to you . . ." making it clear that following Him would mean a realignment of their thinking patterns. If you and I are to grow into His likeness, we must be prepared to break with the status quo, the "you-have-heard-it-said" philosophies of our day and give ourselves to a whole new way of thinking as well.

Paul picked up this same theme when he wrote, "Do not conform any longer to the pattern of this world, but be transformed by the renewing of your mind" (Romans 12:2).

Louie's lexicon tells me the Greek word for *mind* is *nous*, and it doesn't refer to the intellect in a set-apart way, but to the whole person in an "Ah ha! I see it now" kind of knowing. The "mind" changes (is remade) and we begin to understand everything in a very different way. Nothing else may change. The same circumstances and data may be around us but we will see them in a new light. We will have insight and comprehension that we simply never had before.

The key to this change is to personalize the Word. We saw this recently in the life of a man in our congregation . . . a man for whom Christ has become real for the first time this past year. Just before the Christmas holidays, he called Louie's office to see what he might do to help some of the growing number of homeless people in our city. "I know the homeless problem has been with us for a long time," he said, "but I've never really thought much about being my brother's keeper. At least not in a way that had anything to do with me!"

Louie's administrative assistant, Honni Smith, who is a ministering person to the very core of her being and who, along with her husband, Bob, has a heart for needy people that just doesn't stop, knew exactly how to connect this man's desire to help with some very needy people.

So, while the situation was not new, this man's attitude *about* the people caught in the situation was. Because of that, Christmas was different for several hundred homeless people this year who were served a holiday feast as a consequence of one man's new way of thinking.

Paul contends that when our personalization of the Word

occurs in this way, then we ourselves are on the road to change. But it takes time. In the words of Eugene Petersen, it is "a long obedience in the same direction." For as long as we live on earth, we will have the world tugging at us to go one way and our Lord leading us in quite another direction. Again and again, we will have to choose to listen to Jesus Christ when He says, "You have heard it said . . . but *I say to you* . . . ." For in that statement He is asking us to obey His voice above every other. Yes, the remaking of our minds and the transformation of our lives will go on forever. Not until that final day when we are with Christ and we will "know as we are known" will our transformation be complete.

A NEW WAY OF THINKING ABOUT WHO OWNS OUR LIVES

In the meantime, where do we start letting our minds be remade? We must begin with the most basic questions of life:

"Who am I?"

"To whom do I belong?"

Immediately the tug-of-war begins. Our culture would have us believe we belong to ourselves. "Take charge. You're number one. If you don't put yourself first, who will?" the voices ask. "You are the captain of your fate, the master of your soul" and on and on.

Yes, the world does a real job on us, and for the most part, we adapt to its views, either consciously or unconsciously, as though they were our own—until, hopefully, God gets our attention one day, in a way we can't ignore. It may be through a trial, a loss of something or someone very dear, or a time of testing we bring upon ourselves, when we become freshly aware of our own vulnerability.

When life tries us, God uses that experience to challenge us to consider the alternative to a life centered on ourselves. "What is not God's will can nevertheless be God's instrument" is the way Leslie Weatherhead puts it. For it is in our need that we are more ready to learn a new way of thinking, more open to giving up the control and ownership of our lives, and more eager to hear and understand God's plan for us. And we find that plan consistently and clearly given all through Scripture.

"You are meant for Me," God says again and again. About the giving of the Law in Leviticus 20:26, we read, "Ye shall be holy unto me: for I the Lord am holy" (KJV). In Exodus 19:5 we are called God's "peculiar treasure," and the word *peculiar,* from the Latin, means "to have exclusive possession of something." Through the prophet Isaiah, God reminds us we are the people "I formed for myself" (43:21). Then, as we turn to the New Testament, God's claim on our lives is described in the strongest and most compelling of terms:

> He [Christ] died for all, that those who live should no longer live for themselves but for him who died for them.
>
> 2 Corinthians 5:15

> You are not your own; you were bought at a price.
>
> 1 Corinthians 6:19–20

> "Whoever loses his life for my sake will find it."
>
> Matthew 10:39

When the Holy Spirit begins to convince us that there is truth in this, that indeed we are a ransomed, redeemed people; that Jesus doesn't rent us, He owns us; that we are literally His slaves, and as such we do not make plans for our own lives, but we live under His orders.

The result will be a *new* way of thinking and will lead to radical transformation of our lives. When you and I finally believe that we actually *do* belong to God and our lives are meant to honor God, not ourselves, that is precisely what will begin to happen to us. Thinking that new, radical way will go to the very root of who we are and, at that deep level, begin to change us from the inside out.

A NEW WAY OF THINKING ABOUT POSSESSIONS

If I belong to Jesus, then all that I own belongs to Him as well. He will see that my needs are met, and beyond that, He may give me more than I need and ask me, as His servant, to manage that share of His wealth on His behalf (Matthew 25:14–30). But if I begin to think that what belongs to my Master is mine and spend it on myself, totally ignoring His desire for its use, then I am no longer a faithful servant in His likeness. I am an embezzler.

And so the answer to the question "To whom do I belong?" has everything to do with our attitudes about possessions. If we belong to God, that will transform the way we relate to a materialistic society. Growing in the likeness of Jesus in this area can make us very peculiar people. We will be out of step with the world around us.

Some years ago a couple who are among our closest friends came into a lot of money. "I mean, a heap," the wife exclaimed, as the four of us sat on the rooftop porch of our 100-year-old rowhouse in the center of Washington. Relaxing after dinner, we watched the glow of the long summer day give way to the twinkling lights of night all around us. Sitting there with those people we loved so much, I couldn't help but wonder how this new turn of events might change things for them.

Eight years later I can say that their lives have changed astonishingly little. The reason? They had always been good stewards for the Lord, truly believing that whatever they had belonged to their Master. Since over the years they had proved "faithful over little," now God was simply trusting them to be faithful over much. In fact, "a real heap."

And faithful they have been! They still live in the same Washington apartment, still drive the same car, and the truth is, most people would never have a clue that they are stewards over so much. The one difference I see is an intensely joyful glint in their eyes these days, as they watch people being blessed by the foundation they have set up as a vehicle to help people in need. Anonymously, of course! They are "transformed" people in the way they relate to the things of this world and as stewards they have genuinely "entered into the joy of their Master." An experience that could have gotten them offtrack has only served to aid them in their goal of growing in Jesus' likeness.

These friends challenge us! Louie and I live simply, or so we like to think. Our church, which is located in the Embassy Row area of Washington, has a sister relationship with an inner city church. We want to be bridge people and so we live in the city within two and a half miles of the downtown church, considered a high-risk area. Whatever comes to us to use—home, car, whatever—belongs to God. That means that many groups needing a place to meet in our city use our house. Our guest room is full much of the time. *But* every now and then something happens that reveals to us how the world still tugs at our values. Then we discover that we are *not* living as simply or wearing our possessions as loosely as we think.

Some time ago, a small group of friends came to Washington on behalf of a young woman named Carmen. Carmen had gone to a poor and repressive nation in Latin America to do relief work with a Christian organization. Soon after she arrived, she was taken political prisoner without explanation and simply disappeared for a troubling length of time. Her mother and father—who are new citizens of the United States and limited in their English and their funds—and some of Carmen's college friends had come to the capital to work for her release. Amnesty International was helping them, but they needed shelter and a car to get them to their appointments at offices and embassies around town. Hearing of their need from a friend who works with Amnesty, we offered our car for their mission.

At the end of three weeks in Washington, their prayers and advocacy paid off. Carmen was located and released. They were jubilant and we were, too, when they came by the house to return the car and share their good news. Then they were on their way rejoicing.

A story with a happy ending, right? Well, not altogether. Because the next time Louie needed to use the car, he found it in terrible condition. Among other things, the rear brakes were absolutely gone, making a sickening grinding sound.

"Lord," Louie asked, "how could anyone keep driving a car that made a noise like that? Unbelievable!"

You need to know a bit about Louie to understand why he felt the way he did. Louie Evans is mechanical to his fingertips. He can fix just about anything and it delights him to keep a car running for 250,000 miles. He attaches affection to certain material things, not because he is hung up on possessions—he's not!—but because he cares for them so long and so well.

So it hurt him to see a good, old, well-cared-for piece of machinery misused. As he dismantled the brakes and surveyed the damage, I could hear him mutter, "Oh, no! I can't believe this! Why, the brakes are right down to the metal." And finally in utter consternation, "Lord, what have they done to my car?" Then silence.

Louie told me later that as soon as *my car* came from his lips he almost choked on the words. God began to deal with him in a strong way. The message was one of rebuke and it went like an arrow to Louie's heart.

Whose car? I thought we settled that long ago.

Louie's mind flashed back to the many times he had taught the principle of God's ownership of everything to the congregations he had served. Even more, he thought of the times he had actually said, "Lord, all I have is Yours."

Contrite and humbled, Louie turned his thoughts to what the car would need—used drums, new brake shoes, rebuilt cylinder. Hmm, about $250. Then the quiet command, *Fix it!*

Still muttering a bit, Louie did just that. He bought the parts, made the repairs, and finally experienced the satisfaction of driving an old car that ran good-as-new.

A few days later, an unexpected check for $250 arrived in the mail. As owner, God had provided for the car and we had been reminded again that growing in the likeness of our Master means an ever-looser grasp on the things of this world. Louie and I are still very much in process! But we are certain of this truth: When our minds are remade and we understand God's ownership of our lives, it radically changes the way we relate to the things around us.

A NEW WAY OF THINKING ABOUT SUCCESS

It also affects the way we view success. And this is a tough one, for it is right for us to do our tasks well. "Whatever you do, work at it with all your heart . . ." (Colossians 3:23). But when some measure of success comes to us as a result of what we do, it is also right for the honor and praise to be given back to God, where it belongs.

I love the way Dick Halverson, who is in his ninth year as chaplain of the U.S. Senate, has always responded to any thanks or compliment directed at him. He responds with an immediate "Praise the Lord." And from Dick, that is *not* a cliché!

But it is alarmingly easy for most of us to take credit for anything done through us. The success syndrome is inherent in our society, and it has invaded the Christian world, too. Consider how much emphasis is given today to size, numbers, budgets, indexes of growth, a bottom-line bureaucratic mentality. Some of this has to be, and I am genuinely grateful for those who are gifted to work in these areas in a godly, accountable way. But does the numbers game have to be so dominant in our thinking and take up so much of our time and energy?

When quantified success is the goal, there is the danger that individuals or institutions will be tempted to take shortcuts to get where they think they should be and will confuse those results with ministry. "Bottom-line" results are only the handmaid of ministry. Ministry is what happens in the lives of people. Jesus made that clear, and as we are growing in His likeness, that is where our growing emphasis is sure to be . . . with people!

How a Christian views success is not simple, as my friend Harold Bratt reminded me just the other evening. A meeting was suddenly canceled and without needing to check with one another, Louie and I knew what we wanted to do with our free night. We called several special friends we had been wanting to spend some time with and *voilà!* By some miracle they were all free. I found a favorite chicken and water chestnut casserole in the freezer and pulled it out to thaw while I ran to the neighborhood mom-and-pop store for extras. So with a minimum of time and fuss, a company meal was in the works. Back home, Louie laid the fire while I set the table with the blue Wedgewood that Louie's mother had passed on to us, and as I lit the candles, our guests walked through the front door.

And what a wonderful evening it was! Good friends . . . warm and yeasty conversation. In fact, we sat around the table sharing until the fire had lost all its warmth and the candles were nothing but stubs. It was a special night, and two of the people who made it so were Harold and JoAnne Bratt, who have spent much of their lives together serving the federal government including tours overseas with the State Department.

I had been sitting next to Harold during dinner when our conversation turned to the way a Christian views success. A few days later, a thoughtful letter arrived from him. I found what he had to say so challenging that I've asked his permission to share some of his thinking with you.

"I can in good conscience affirm how screwed up are the values of the world and how they should be replaced by Christ's. At the same time I'm affirming this view, however, I'm enjoying the fruits of men and women who doubtless worked and lived according to the standards of the world seeking fame and fortune.

"Take the entrepreneur whose enslavement to work and accumulation of capital contribute so mightily to the driving of our private enterprise economy. We all enjoy the products his slavery and drive provide. How can we Christians rationalize our enjoyment of the benefits we receive from this kind of behavior and at the same time radically challenge the values that, frankly, make modern life possible?

"I'm a graduate of a Christian college and in perusing its alumni bulletin I'm hard-pressed to see where its standards are very different from those of a secular institution. Alumni notes often refer to someone who has been promoted to a higher or more influential position or whose work has been recognized by secular authorities. I think Christian colleges are generally proud of the 'worldly achievements' of their graduates.

"I don't have any answers, but I guess I'm coming down more on the importance of *doing well* here as well as *doing good*. I hope one can do well . . . without adopting all the false standards and criteria of the world."

I agree with Harold that it is possible to do both "well" and "good" without adopting the false standards of the world. At the same time, I am convinced that while a Christian may enjoy success, success should never be the Christian's goal. Not if our goal is to grow into the likeness of Jesus, for divided loyalties stunt spiritual growth. (Matthew 6:24 says it as it is: We cannot serve two masters! Not should not, but cannot.)

I still cherish the statement made by Mother Teresa when she was visiting Washington some years ago:

"God has never called us to be successful, only faithful."

Success, as the world sees it, may or may not come to us in this life. That is not very important, actually. What really

matters is that we are faithful to God, no matter what comes
to us . . . and that in all things, our lives give glory to God.

This is indeed a new way of thinking!

A NEW WAY OF THINKING
ABOUT OUR ENEMIES

Jesus also charts a new direction for us in terms of the way
we relate to people. Just read Matthew 5, beginning with
verse 21, and see how often Jesus said, "You have heard it
said . . . but *I* say to you . . ." and then mark the number of
times the "*I* say to you" has to do with the way we treat
people.

If we look closely at just one section, for example, the
passage that deals with the way disciples are to treat their
enemies, we can see how radical this new way of thinking
and being really is:

> "If someone strikes you on the right cheek, turn to him the other
> also. And if someone wants to sue you and take your tunic, let him
> have your cloak as well. If someone forces you to go one mile, go
> with him two miles. . . . Love your enemies and pray for those who
> persecute you. . . ."   Matthew 5:39–41, 44

The King James Version puts it: "Do good to them that
hate you, and pray for them which despitefully use you"
(verse 44).

Radical indeed! I know people whose lives have been
transformed to the place where they are actually living this
way! I think of one friend who has been the object of a cruel
takeover coup of his business. Rejected, he is nevertheless
praying for some way to minister to the man who master-
minded the ugly episode. And we have seen him grow more

like Christ through this painful experience than we have in all the previous years we have known him.

And I remember Edith,* a committed woman who, a decade ago, was abandoned by her husband for a younger woman he met while working in the Orient, a woman he eventually married. When Edith heard that her ex-husband had died, leaving this young widow and two small children penniless, she felt compassion on their behalf. One day as she was praying for them, God impressed on her mind a way that she could "do good" for the one who had "despitefully used" her. She could open her home to the family that was part of the man she had loved for so long. And that was what she determined to do. At least she would make the offer and the rest she would leave to the Lord.

I'm sure there was apprehension in Edith's heart as she wrote the letter of invitation and then waited for the response. But as she dropped that letter in the mailbox Edith took a step toward growing in the likeness of her Master. Her radical invitation and her investment of love in the years since have paid deeply satisfying dividends! Edith and the younger woman live harmoniously together and the little girls have grown and flourished in an atmosphere of warmth and affection. The real miracle, from what I understand, is that Edith feels life has been given back to her as she has come to cherish not only the children, but the gentle woman her husband loved and left her for.

I don't know about you, but that kind of love hits me in a very tender place. When the radical love of Jesus is lived out, everyone wins!

————

* I first read Edith's story in *Guideposts*.

A NEW WAY OF THINKING IN THE LIKENESS OF CHRIST

"Be transformed by the renewing of your mind." The more I focus on this verse, the more I see the need for "renewed minds" in our world today.

I'm convinced that our minds can be renewed when we become Kingdom thinkers with the criterion for every decision being "How will this affect the Kingdom of God?" This is the way Jesus thought. He came only to do the will of His Father. Again and again He broke with tradition and culture and encouraged a whole new way of thinking with His "But I say to you." Jesus saw everything from a Kingdom point of view.

Jesus had a magnificent obsession, the Kingdom of God. He lived for it and He died for it—and He wants us to share that obsession with Him. This will mean the renewing of our minds, the total realignment of our priorities—thinking about everything in a new way.

Question Ideas

1. Describe how the world has trained you to think that you are in control of your own life.

2. How does that conflict with God's way for you?

3. If God owns you, what does that say about your possessions and about the people in your life?

4. In your own life what is the main place of struggle between cultural conditioning and God's "new way of thinking"?

5. Where have you broken with the status quo?

8

. . . And in Our Relationships

We have been watching Jesus' nature and personality unfold before us as we find Him in the Word, in acts of trust and obedience, in *agape* love, in our very thoughts.

And certainly we will find Him in friendships.

How well I remember when it first struck me that Jesus lives in relationships. It began early one sleepless morning in my nineteenth year when I responded to Jesus' invitation "Come to Me." I didn't understand theology and knew absolutely no Christian jargon. All I knew was that God was seeking entrance into my life through Jesus Christ and I was saying yes, whatever that meant.

There was no dramatic experience that accompanied my submission to Jesus Christ, only a profound sense of union. But later, as I entered my busy world of people, I was aware of a strong sense of compassion for others, a new connectedness to every person I met. It was amazing! I didn't know the verse "But now in Christ Jesus you who once were far away have been brought near through the blood of Christ" (Ephesians 2:13), but that was my experience that day.

It was the beginning of my experience of finding Jesus, actually beholding Him, in relationships.

It's true, isn't it? Once connected to the Vine, we are connected to all the other branches. Jesus cannot be separated from the *working* out and *living* out of our relationships because He is in them. As Paul Bunyan reminds us, "Christianity is not a solitary religion."

While Jesus is to be found in the midst of all relationships—casual, political, religious, supportive, even hostile—what intrigues me most is watching Jesus with His friends.

In His few short years on this earth, Jesus was so totally human that He experienced every longing of our hearts. And one of those longings was for close personal relationships—people with whom He could share His life.

Jesus needed friends! In Mark 3:14, at the very beginning of His public ministry, we read that Jesus chose twelve "that they might be with him." Among the twelve there were three to whom He felt especially close, and among the three, John was singled out as "the disciple Jesus loved" in a special way. There were others, of course—Mary, Martha, Lazarus, "the other Mary," and more, all of which emphasizes that if we want to behold Jesus, one important way to do so is in our friendships.

As we study the way He related to His friends, we will see just how important those relationships were to Him. We will also discover much about making our own relationships more meaningful as we watch and learn from His example.

BEATITUDES OF FRIENDSHIP

Looking at certain key relationships Jesus had with people, I see some specific characteristics emerge—characteristics that coincide amazingly with the "covenants" Louie has listed in his splendid little book on small groups, *Covenant to Care*. (The comparison is really not amazing since Louie drew his covenants from the life of Jesus as well!) I would like to discuss these characteristics in the form of "The *Be*atitudes of Friendship." We will see how Jesus has anointed friendship as a way to grow in His likeness.

1. Be Available

Jesus, the One through whom the Holy Spirit is now equally available to all at all times, was not able to give Himself to all people equally during His years on earth. He knew the same limits of time and space that we know and so He had to make the same difficult decisions we do as to how and with whom He would spend His days. Jesus chose to give priority to His disciples, whom He called "My friends." At times Jesus would leave the multitudes to be alone with them. They had hundreds of unrecorded conversations as they walked along the dusty roads of Jerusalem and Galilee. We know from what has been recorded that Jesus spent hours teaching His disciples on hillsides, in gardens, around tables, and in an upper room in Jerusalem.

There were others to whom Jesus assigned priority— Mary, Martha, and Lazarus—whose home seemed to be a favorite respite for Him as He walked the two miles southeast of Jerusalem, through Bethany.

Jesus knew that friends take time. Most of us don't have the kind of time that quality relationships require unless we make deep friendships a priority. This will mean building time into our schedules for the people with whom we think God wants us to share our lives.

Louie and I have a small band of friends here in Washington, brothers and sisters who have become family to us. Once a year, looking months ahead, we circle dates to make sure we will have time for each other. Once those times are set, barring real emergencies, they are priority. For more than twelve years we have been a support group—laughing, crying, struggling, playing, praying, and generally keeping one another honest in our walks with Christ.

Of course, we are not perfect friends to one another, because we are not perfect people! We hurt, disappoint, and are not always there for everyone when we should be, but we have learned to be very "straight" with one another about our feelings and to forgive one another for human frailty. Sharing our joy and pain has become enormously important to us. I am reminded of an occasion when, after a bout with hepatitis, Louie was deeply weary and discouraged. Our covenant brothers and sisters met with us, prayed with us, encouraged us; they literally loved Louie back into ministry. I'll never forget that!

To be available means time and presence. It also means to be with people in terms of our attention and our willingness to listen. Perhaps one of the greatest gifts we can give as friends is to be available to one another through a pair of sensitive, listening ears. Growing in Jesus' likeness will mean being *available* to friends—making commitments just as Jesus did.

2. Be Affirming

In all His relationships, Jesus looked for the potential in every person. Much like the fictional Don Quixote, Jesus could see beyond the surface and call forth beautiful new possibilities from people. He saw good in a man called Matthew who was part of a hated breed of tax collectors. He saw beyond a vacillating fisherman called Simon to the man who became "Peter the rock." He saw a purity of love and motivation that others did not recognize in Mary Magdalene, a woman who had spent most of her life giving away misguided love.

Almost immediately His followers began to emulate His

model of affirmation. The apostle Paul wrote this advice to the church at Philippi: "Whatever is true, whatever is noble, whatever is right, whatever is pure, whatever is lovely, whatever is admirable—if anything is excellent or praiseworthy—think about such things."

Then there was Barnabas, remembered primarily because he was such an encourager to others. Remember the way he defended Paul before the church in Jerusalem when no one seemed to be in his corner cheering? And it was Barnabas who encouraged Paul to return to his ministry after a period of self-imposed exile. Later Barnabas became the advocate for John Mark when Paul had some reservations about the younger man. I can't help but wonder how many ministries have been saved over the years by a faithful "Barnabas" type who was at the right place at the right time, to defend and encourage a maligned servant of the Lord. I know that Louie and I have often thanked God for the "Barnabases" in our lives!

Affirming friends can see something in us that we are not able to see in ourselves. That is why many of us do not discover our strongest gifts except through others. Surely God wants each of us to be a "Barnabas" for someone! "Consider how we may spur one another on toward love and good deeds" (Hebrews 10:24). *Be affirming.* Jesus was. Growing in His likeness will mean we, too, will become more and more encouraging of others.

3. Be Generous

Jesus said, "Blessed are the merciful, the generous people." He not only said it, He lived it in all His relationships. To be generous is to be loving, forgiving, not to hold grudges or keep a record of misdeeds. The "be generous" attitude means we will not be prickly and faultfinding with our friends. Besides, the things that drive us crazy in others are usually the very things we dislike in ourselves. Jesus tells us that a judging attitude is risky business because the speck we see in our sister's or brother's eye is really a reflection of the log in our own eye. So we need to be generous, loving, forgiving of the slights and misunderstandings that occur in any close, intimate relationship. When we are not forgiving toward others, it really implies that we don't feel we need God's forgiveness in our own lives. "Bear with each other and forgive whatever grievances you may have against one another. Forgive as the Lord forgave you" (Colossians 3:13).

But what about the friend who turns her back on you, perhaps even betrays you? What about the friend who becomes "the enemy"?

Jesus gives us the answer, again from His own life and teaching. In the chapter on love we saw how, on the very day Judas was to betray Him, Jesus in an act of servanthood washed his feet, leaving for us the ultimate example of how we are to treat our betrayers. "If you love those who love you, what reward will you get? Are not even the tax collectors doing that?" (Matthew 5:46).

This kind of generosity toward friends who have turned on us is foolishness to the world. When Jesus says, "If someone hits you on one cheek, turn to him the other also," the world shouts, "No way. Hit back or you'll get walked all over!" But this is one of the many ways Christians are peculiar, different from the world. For us, not hitting back is a sign that we are growing in the likeness of our Master. I love the way Oswald Chambers puts it: "For the saint, personal insult becomes the occasion of revealing the incredible sweetness of the Lord Jesus."

No one says following Jesus across secure lines into enemy

territory will be easy, but the world will know more about our faith by the way we deal with the friend who betrays us than by the way we respond to the friend who loves us. *Be generous!* Growing in the likeness of Jesus will lead us to generosity.

4. Be Prayerful At Times of Crisis

During His last night on earth when death came rattling at Jesus' door, He was so very human. He didn't want to go through the upcoming ordeal and we can all identify with that. Jesus struggled with death. "Father, if you are willing, take this cup from me" (Luke 22:42). During His last night He sought the strength and company of His Father in prayer. But that wasn't all. He also asked for the company of three friends.

Matthew recorded for us, some 35 years after that night, that Jesus took with Him Peter, James, and John and said to them, "My soul is overwhelmed with sorrow to the point of death. Stay here and keep watch with me" (Matthew 26:38).

In His time of need, Jesus was asking for the company, support, and prayers of His closest friends. It is sad that they fell asleep, but the truth that Jesus wanted them near Him is not diminished by their very human response. In our times of need we would do well to follow His example—to seek the company of God the Father and our most trusted friends.

Many times during the past 35 years Louie and I have "kept watch" over one another as we have prayed through the "Gethsemanes" of life together. And often, during those times, we have felt the need for other covenant sisters and brothers to join us. I think of a crisis that occurred in our lives some years ago when a series of losses left us wounded and hurting. Then some dear friends who were vacationing 3,000 miles away happened to call one night to check in on us. When they learned of the situation we were wrestling with they immediately flew home to "keep watch with us," and to help pray us through a difficult time. Can you imagine how much that meant to us? I choke up thinking about it even now after all the years. (In fact, I think I will call them tonight!)

Jesus prayed for His friends, too. Remember when He told Peter, "Simon, Simon, behold, Satan has demanded permission to sift you like wheat; but I have prayed for you" (Luke 22:31–32, NAS)? There are some who feel that prayer is not practical: "Give a person your presence, not your prayers." But if anyone's presence would have been sufficient to meet the needs of another human being, it would have been the presence of Jesus Christ. Jesus was *with* Peter and yet He also *prayed* for him.

The scriptural evidence is clear! As people pray for one another in Christ's name and in line with His will, there is strength and power unleashed that is not otherwise given. Growing in the likeness of Jesus means asking our friends to pray with us in our dark hours, just as He did! "Come, watch with me."

5. Be Vulnerable

If you have bought into the cultural philosophy that each one of us should be able to make it on our own, this beatitude is exceedingly important. To grow in the likeness of Jesus will mean a transformation, a journey into vulnerability.

We have seen how forthright Jesus was with His close friends about His struggle with death in the Garden of Gethsemane. Could He have been any more open than when He said, "I am grieved to the point of death. Stay with me"? How human and honest He was with them about His desire to have them near.

And there are many other instances in the Gospels where Jesus showed a natural openness about His needs. Remember the story of Jesus waiting at Jacob's well in the city of Samaria (John 4:5–8)? Somehow He let His disciples know He was tired, "weary from the journey," too tired to go get food. Or perhaps one of the disciples noticed a look of fatigue on His face and said, "Master, You rest here by the well while we go get food." Whatever, Jesus didn't hide His weariness from His friends.

The point is this: In the way He lived His life, Jesus gave us permission to be vulnerable and open about our needs. In our times of fear, grief, weariness, *we are not meant to struggle alone.* Jesus is always available to us through the Holy Spirit. And there are others waiting for us to say, "I need you." Jesus intends us to reach out, as He did, to a few trusted friends. In these special friendships we behold the Master Himself. Growing in His likeness will mean becoming open and vulnerable, as Jesus was, with our friends.

6. Be Sensitive

Jesus was always sensitive to people. When the rich young ruler couldn't meet the costly requirements of discipleship, Jesus respected him too much to chase after him. He never demeaned the poor by lumping them into categories; He always personalized need. As someone has said, "Jesus treated the least of these as though they were the most!"

The Gospels are bursting with examples of Jesus' sensitivity. I love the story of the sinful woman who sought out Jesus in the home of a Pharisee, flung herself weeping at His feet, wet His feet with her tears and some ointment, then wiped them with the hairs of her head. The house of a Pharisee was no place for her—a woman of the streets! And using long, flowing hair to wipe the Master's feet had every eyebrow raised, for no proper woman in that culture would wear her hair loose and uncovered in public.

How did Jesus react to this bizarre demonstration? He didn't try to stop her. He didn't seem to be the least bit embarrassed by her actions. He saw something within her that touched His heart: a boldness of spirit, a capacity for affection, and a desperate need for the right kind of love in her life. In response to her need, Jesus said to His judgmental host, " 'Her many sins have been forgiven—for she loved much.' . . . Jesus said to her, 'Your sins are forgiven' " (Luke 7:47–48).

I can't help but think how differently that story might have ended if Jesus had not been sensitive to the need inside that woman. This story tells us that it is not uncommon for people to exhibit deep needs in strange outward behavior. Yet how often I see a person's outward actions and never get beyond them to what's really going on inside.

I'm thinking of a friend who has become a very critical, judging, gossipy person of late. I tend to get exasperated with her, but I sense the need to take a deeper look. Not that I should condone her gossip, for it is hurting too many people. But I have a conviction that her bitterness springs from loneliness and bad feelings about herself. Her harsh, "mad-at-everybody" attitude may just be her way of waving a flag of distress that signals, "Help me! Love me! See my need!"

Jesus, help me to be more sensitive, like You! To grow in Your likeness means to look beyond the surface and care about the real person inside, just as You did.

7. Be Accountable

Jesus was accountable to God. We see that so clearly in His Garden prayer: "O my Father, if it be possible, let this cup pass from me: nevertheless, not as I will, but as thou wilt" (Matthew 26:39, KJV). That *nevertheless* says it all. Nothing was more important to Jesus than doing the will of God.

Following in the likeness of Jesus, Paul the apostle was accountable to God on behalf of the people who were entrusted to his care. Paul wrote to the Philippians, "I desire to depart and be with Christ . . . but it is more necessary for you that I remain in the body. Convinced of this, I know that I will remain, and I will continue with all of you, for your progress and joy in the faith" (Philippians 1:23–25).

In his book on covenant relationships, Louie puts it clearly: "Accountability means this—what happens to you matters to me." As disciples of Christ, our accountability is first to Him, and then to one another.

In his book *Rebuilding Your Broken World* Gordon MacDonald has an insightful section on the importance of building accountability into our relationships. Written from a private crucible of failure and despair, he moves into repentance, forgiveness, grace, and hope. Along the way he offers the warning that "most of our lives today move at such a fast pace that, sadly, many of us lack the kind of personal relationships that give accountability where we provide balance, nourishment, and honest feedback for one another." And, "most of us live far from our extended families and move so swiftly there are few people—if any—who know us deeply."

The truth is that we need the help of others. We need friends who will be there for us over the long haul—people who love us enough to hold us to godly standards and encourage us to grow in the likeness of Christ. We must be intentional about developing and putting aside the time for some very special relationships, in which mutual accountability is agreed upon up front, in which we say to one another, "What happens to you matters to me," and mean it.

For those of us who are married, this kind of holy accountability should begin with our spouses, the number one priority in terms of human relationships. Then, like good leaven, accountability spreads from husband and wife to parents and children. How much we need to affirm and encourage one another within the family. But that isn't all. We also need to discipline, correct, and ask the tough questions of one another in order to become the people God wants us to be. If we love our children, we will do this for them and, as they grow and mature, they will do the same for us.

I remember when Jamie, our youngest son, came home from seminary just after we'd moved from a house in Maryland to our much smaller row house in the city. I was delighted to have Jamie home for many reasons, but one was the fact that he is such a good and willing worker, and I had lots of work to get done. At 6′3″ and 190 pounds of brawn, he could trot those big heavy boxes up and down the stairs as though they were filled with nothing but air.

So the first morning we met in the kitchen after breakfast and I said, "Now, Jamie, today how about if you and I do this. . . ." And Jamie followed directions and did it all.

The next day, the same situation. "Jamie, today I think it would be good if you and I did thus and so. . . ." And again Jamie did all the heavy work I needed done without a word of protest.

But on the third morning, as I was about to rehearse the same scene, Jamie held up his arms and said, "Whoa, Mom!

Wait just a minute. I don't mind doing this stuff—I'm glad to. But when you keep saying, 'Jamie, how about you and I,' you really mean, 'Jamie, how about *you!*' Let's just be straight with each other and say it as it is, O.K.?"

And Jamie was right. He was keeping me accountable to a principle we had tried to teach all the kids through the years—something I believed but had forgotten for the moment. A small thing? Perhaps, but being transparent and straight in relationships *is* important! And it starts with little things.

I'm glad Jamie spoke up. In fact, I'm glad all of our children speak up when they feel they need to. It's a gift they give us.

Recently, Louie and I had a decision to make and after praying about it, we went to our growing family of children for their counsel. We're always a lively group when we get together. But this night was particularly yeasty with animated discussion, probing questions, prayer, and at evening's end, some very wise and perceptive advice. Later, as we were getting ready for bed, Louie said, "Wow, are we rich! Our kids are our best counselors!"

He's right! They know us, love us, want God's best for us, and they will talk straight with us. What more could we ask? Yes, accountability should start at home where, like God, we love one another just as we are, but also like God, we love too much to leave one another "just as we are." We want to encourage one another to keep growing. That's accountability!

I'm fortunate to have family who will do this for me, but it doesn't stop there. I have already mentioned the covenant group that means so much to Louie and me. Within that group there are several with whom I have made a specific covenant of mutual accountability. And there is one person in particular who knows me so well she can often recognize signs of stress in me long before I am aware of them myself. When she comes to me, looks me in the eye, and says, "Coke, I love you but there's something I must say to you," believe me, I listen. She has earned the right to speak to me and I give her that permission in my life. We do it for each other because it matters. It *really* does.

Catherine Marshall LeSourd was that kind of friend to me. How I valued her honesty and the way she would call and ask, for instance, in reference to my writing, "Coke, are you *abiding* in your call?" She kept me accountable in more ways than one!

In the section of *Rebuilding Your Broken World* dealing with this subject, Gordon MacDonald offers practical suggestions for those of us who want relationships that include mutual accountability. He writes, "How do we protect one another? We watch a friend's eyes. Abnormal fatigue? Anger? Avoidance of truth? We listen to a friend's words to lovingly discern inconsistencies, attitudes, and negative criticisms of people. We watch spending patterns. Too excessive? Trying to prove something? We note the respect and affection with which he or she treats others. Loving toward a spouse and children? Too harsh? Disdainful? Disrespectful? Too familiar with others? We are sensitive to questionable habits. Substance abuse? Sleeplessness? Workaholism? I am not advocating that we adopt a KGB-like stance toward one another. But men and women who truly love one another protect one another from broken world possibilities." Gordon is right.

So is Bunyan when he says, "Christianity is not a solitary religion." And people who encourage us in our spiritual journey and who share a common goal can be incredible agents of change on our behalf. But they also do this by being tough with us, speaking the truth in love, and keeping us honest and accountable.

Let's thank God for the people who care enough to be His loving instruments of transformation in our lives. They could well be the angels God sends to help us toward our goal: the likeness of Jesus Christ in all our relationships.

Question Ideas

1. Why do you think Jesus asked twelve people to "be with Him" during His ministry?

2. Does the fact that He gave a time priority to certain chosen friends free you to do the same?

3. In what ways do people who know you and care for you deeply keep you accountable? Do they give you permission to do the same for them?

4. In what ways are speaking and hearing the truth in love difficult for you? Explain.

5. As you grow in the likeness of Jesus, are your relationships with others growing as well?

9

Following Jesus Across Cultural Lines

Louie and I had been in Africa for two weeks and were now visiting a village out in the Zimbabwe bush, where World Vision, in partnership with the people residing in the area, sponsors a child survival project.

It was there I met her. We were both wives and mothers, but beyond those ties, every external circumstance of our lives separated us from one another. I was white, old enough to be her mother. She was young and beautiful, her skin a rich glowing ebony. For a while I watched her gather pumpkins from her garden just outside the mud-thatched hut where she lived with her husband and two small children. Then our eyes met and she came to me. We sat side by side. Separated by nation, race, language, generation, and culture, we nevertheless spoke to one another in ways too deep for words. Our hands and eyes met and we understood that in some mystical way we were one. We were sisters in Christ, bound together by life's strongest bond.

Later that night, back at the hotel, I spoke to Louie of that meeting and he smiled. He understood, for he has had that same experience many times—an instant bonding of two lives through the Holy Spirit. For days I saw her lovely face before me—a symbol of the unity that can exist across all lines. It was just a moment in our lives and yet it expressed the reality of Paul's words to the Ephesians: "Now in Christ Jesus you who once were far away [from God and one another] have been brought near through the blood of Christ" (2:13).

In recent years the unity that comes when life's external barriers are removed has become increasingly significant to me. God has been doing some hefty reshaping in this area of my life. I now see that when I take any step or adopt any attitude that separates me from God's people, I grieve the Spirit. And I inhibit the process of growing in His likeness. For Christ destroyed those barriers and when I rebuild them, I sin; I mock the cross on which He died.

CROSSING THE LINES JESUS CROSSED

I want to grow in the likeness of Jesus, so I *must* grow in my openness to all kinds of people. This is the way Jesus lived. He calls us to follow Him across every cultural line to that place of oneness in Him for which He paid so dearly.

Consider His life. Jesus was a rebel in the way He broke the rules. Not God's rules—those He lived out beautifully and fulfilled. But the manmade rules that governed the culture of His time, those He broke again and again.

You see, a good, religious Jewish man just didn't eat meals with known sinners, befriend tax collectors, visit with women and treat them as equals, offer dignity to foreign and hated Samaritans, touch fearsome lepers, or heal a hurting person on the Sabbath.

But Jesus did. And through His example He is today urging His disciples to live boldly, to take the risk of being rebels as we follow Him across the same cultural lines that He crossed.

Listen to the way The Living Bible records Paul's words

in Colossians 3:11: "In this new life [in Christ] one's nationality or race or education or social position is unimportant; such things mean nothing. Whether a person has Christ is what matters, and he is equally available to all."

In Galatians 3:28, Paul continues that line of thinking when he says, "There is neither Jew nor Greek, slave nor free, male nor female, for you are all one in Christ Jesus." And Jesus asked in His longest recorded prayer (John 17) that we might all become "one" in Him!

If we take those words seriously, they will lead us to freedom and equality today. We have our own cultural lines to cross, whatever they might be, because that is part of our new life in Christ.

For my own growth, I took a close look at Colossians 3:11 to identify some of the cultural lines Scripture admonishes me to cross, and I saw, in that one verse, the lines of 1) nation, 2) race, 3) education, and 4) social position. Then I added a few of my own. Economics, denominationalism (religious style), pet cultural peeves and dislikes, and specifically, *my* challenge: reverse snobbery. You see, I tend to look down on people who look down on people, and I have to be aware of the walls *that* can build.

So let's take a look at these areas of cultural division that affect most of our lives to see where we are in respect to where God wants us to be.

CROSSING THE LINE OF NATIONAL AND POLITICAL DIFFERENCE

When we give ourselves to the process of growing in the likeness of Christ, we must become world-view Christians. This requires a struggle, and it is never easy. Peter's battle to break away from his parochial view of foreigners is recorded in the tenth chapter of Acts. "You know how unlawful it is for a Jew to associate with anyone from another nation," he said on entering the Roman's home to which God had sent him. His struggle is often our struggle and we need to work it through as Peter had to until we can declare with him, "But God has shown me I should not call anyone common or unclean."

I recall with sadness an experience I had not long ago. I was working on a project to provide food for a community of hungry, homeless people who represented a small ethnic group within our city. A lovely, warmhearted friend was helping me until her husband realized what she was doing and put the kibosh on her involvement. He didn't like "all those foreigners" coming into the United States. To him, their hunger and homelessness was a problem and an embarrassment to the nation.

I have to wonder what Jesus would say about this. When He gave us the mandate to welcome the stranger, feed the hungry, and clothe the naked, did He mean for us to make sure first that they agreed with us politically? And to make sure they had done everything possible to help themselves before we extended the cup of cold water in His name? I cannot separate this obedience to Jesus' clear command from the goal of growing in His likeness.

THE LINES OF RACE

Some time ago, I was reading a collection of writings by Martin Luther King, Jr. Regarding the building of relationships across racial lines, he said, "This is not an obstacle to overcome, but an opportunity to participate in the beauty of diversity in Christ."

I agree with my whole heart. Since moving to Washington, D.C., where every nation and racial group is represented and where 75 percent of the residents are black, Louie and I feel that our lives have been enriched beyond measure as we have "participated in the diversity in Christ."

The friendships we have made with neighbors and the covenant relationship we have with Sam and Vicky Hines and their Third Street Church of God family are among the richest we have ever known. We have learned so much about the unity God means for us to have across all racial lines—yet we feel we have only begun to experience what God intends for us in this area of opportunity. He alone knows what lies ahead, but as Sam has said many times, "This love and oneness that we share is so unique, only God could be its source."

In May 1986, when Billy Graham held his crusade in the Greater Washington area, night after night he urged that great diverse gathering to reach out and get to know one another as brothers and sisters across racial lines. It was significant to me that he always did this at the close of the evening as he was inviting those who wanted to commit their lives to Christ to come forward. It was as though Billy was agreeing with the apostle Paul when he wrote, "This is part of your new life in Christ."

How different it is when we get to know people as *people* and not as categories. Recently I was asked to give a brief talk to a group of women characterized by their narrow stand on issues. It seemed to me an opportunity to cross another line. As I shared with them, I told a story from the life of one of my Washington, D.C., sisters that I thought was appropriate to my subject. At the close of the meeting, a woman who knew me *and* my "sister" chided me, saying,

"Your friend is black, but you didn't mention that. Were you afraid to say it to this audience?"

That stopped me for a moment. Why hadn't I? Then I realized that I hadn't mentioned her color because I no longer think about her that way. She is my *friend* friend—not my *black* friend. Long ago, I'm sure, she gave up thinking of me as her *white* friend. Through the years, as we have shared mutual interests and concerns for our often-overworked pastor-husbands, as we have laughed and cried together, as we have prayed together for our children, as we have worked side by side at the breakfasts for the homeless, someplace along the line we stopped seeing one another as "colored" and "colorless" and saw one another for what we truly are—sisters "oned" in Christ.

Not that our relationship has become what it is without cost. I know my friend sometimes takes flak from her closely knit ethnic community for venturing beyond those lines to extend friendship to me. She seems willing to pay the price, however, perhaps because she believes, as I do, that becoming color-blind is one of the side effects we can expect to develop when we are in the process of growing in the likeness of Christ.

CROSSING THE LINES OF ECONOMICS, EDUCATION, AND SOCIAL POSITION

Paul says, "In this new life one's nationality or race or education or social position is unimportant; such things mean nothing. Whether a person has Christ is what matters, and he is equally available to all" (Colossians 3:11, TLB).

I can just hear someone say, "Oh, come now! It's only natural to want to be with people who have the same economic and social background. That's just the way we humans are. Birds of a feather and all that."

I know. We have all been conditioned to think this way. And, of course, we should have friends with whom we have much in common. We should not, however, be *limited* to those relationships that fall within a comfortable, familiar circle. Admittedly, this is easier to talk about than to live out. Most of us have taken on the world's exclusive attitudes, and when our faith calls us to break down barriers, it is not easy to change. Yet we must. And I have found that in the process of changing it is good to remember that our Lord lived most of His life among the poor, that He came from the wrong village ("Can anything good come from Nazareth?"), with the wrong pedigree (conceived out of wedlock), with no formal educational background, and with definitely the wrong accent to make it in Jerusalem.

What is more, as I read the Gospels, I am touched by the way Jesus gives every person He meets the dignity of being taken seriously. No one is judged as "common or unclean." A long, thoughtful look at the way Jesus valued people and related to them without respect to race, gender, or position helps me see the direction and distance I have yet to go. For instance, I notice that He doesn't lump people together in groups as I am prone to do. Nowhere do I find Him speculating about how many poor people there are in Judea living below the poverty level. I'm sure He cared about that but He always personalized need by caring genuinely about the *person* in need.

This convicts me. I care about conditions in Washington and I try to keep abreast of the statistics, trends, and polls. Yet I can forget with alarming ease about my neighbors at the end of the block who are facing eviction because they cannot afford the rent. Vicky and Sam have had efficiency apartments in the same row house for more than forty years. They are the neighborhood historians. They belong here. They have lived in the community all of their lives and they want to stay. Yet simple economics will force them out unless some group cares enough to do something about the lack of decent, low-income housing in our cities. Vicky and Sam, and others like them, help me move away from my conditioning as a sociology major in college where we talked about the needy as categories rather than as people with names and faces, people I have learned to know and care about.

The simplicity of Jesus' life did not set up barriers between Himself and others. He spoke Aramaic, the language of the people, not the Greek that could have set Him apart as culturally privileged. He had the common touch and "common people heard Him gladly." That doesn't mean, however, that He looked askance at those who were rich and powerful.

As I read the exchange in Mark 10:17–22 between Jesus and the rich young ruler who came to Him by night to have a confidential talk, I sense that Jesus really cared about that man. Not for his money, but for himself. And when the young ruler was not able to make the commitment Jesus asked of him, Scripture tells us "he went away sad, because he had great wealth." It also says that "Jesus loved him," and I think He must also have gone from that meeting filled with sorrow. Yet He didn't pursue the man because he was rich, nor did He lower the standards of the Kingdom to add one with his power and status to the disciple band. Jesus honored the rich young ruler's decision, although my heart tells me He grieved as He watched him walk away. Jesus crossed lines in all directions and, following Him, so will we.

CROSSING THE LINES OF DENOMINATION AND RELIGIOUS STYLE

Growing in the likeness of Jesus will mean changing the way we see people and learning to view them as God does. No more pigeon-holing people by sex, age, race, marriage, or singleness. No more categorizing people as rich or poor, socially acceptable or unacceptable. And within the Christian community, no more looking askance at certain groups because of our rigid denominationalism or different traditions and religious styles. To do it Christ's way means we will not classify.

A friend I will simply call Jim and his wife minister in the suburbs of a city known for its mix of people from every background. He and his wife love this diversity, but there was one man named Clyde who was so "far out" in the way he expressed his faith that Jim considered him a religious nut. As a pastor, Jim resented the bad impression that he thought this man made for the Gospel. Dressed in a bizarre way, Clyde carried a gaudy sandwich board plastered with Bible verses and religious slogans. Every time Jim saw this man walking the sidewalks of the city, he flinched and crossed the street to avoid him.

Then something happened in Jim's life. As the result of a personal need, he reached out to God in a new way. He stopped being *religious* and became deeply *spiritual*. That experience changed many of his attitudes.

The next time he went into the city, whom did he see coming toward him but the sandwich board man. Jim thought, *There isn't enough time to cross the street. I'll just look the other way.*

But as the two men drew closer, their eyes met. In that

gaze, Jim realized how much God had changed him. Instead of hostility Jim felt love for Clyde—a love so unique, he knew it had come from God. Here was his spiritual brother . . . they were members of the same Christian family. No words were exchanged when they passed, but as Jim paused to watch his brother make his way up the sidewalk he saw for the first time what was written on the back of the sandwich board. It said, *This is Clyde's way of witnessing. What is yours?*

Our friend Jim found a new freedom when those walls tumbled down around him. He found that following Jesus across cultural lines is no grim duty; it is a joy, even fun!

I remember a moment that occurred when Louie and I were participating in a renewal celebration in New Orleans along with 40,000 people from just about every denomination and nation of the world. The one uniting factor was Jesus Christ, and the common language spoken was love. One night after the evening service while we were making our way out of the sports arena, an elderly Roman Catholic sister, in full habit, came walking toward us. We were still singing the last "hallelujahs" of the closing hymn as we approached one another. Our eyes met and, looking me straight in the eye, she creased her lovely, weathered face into a smile. Suddenly she flung open her arms and threw me a kiss before disappearing into the crowd.

It was only a moment but it is etched on my mind—a tiny gem in my memory bank to remind me that "now in Christ Jesus [we] who once were far away have been brought near through the blood of Christ" (Ephesians 2:13).

Albert Schweitzer once said, "There is so much coldness in the world because we [Christians] are afraid to be as cordial as we really are." How true! We are too often afraid to let the good things we feel toward others show. The older

I get the more I pray God would free me to express the love He has put in my heart for others. I am convinced that spontaneous expressions of affection can go a long way in breaking down the walls we have allowed to surround our lives and separate us from our brothers and sisters in Christ.

The world is weary of watching Christians isolate themselves from one another because of differing beliefs and practices. If we really choose to grow in His likeness, the world *will* see us reaching out for one another, ignoring, as Jesus did, the cultural lines that separate us. What if the world could see people of every nation—black and white, rich and poor, male and female, powerful and powerless, young and old, all God's rich, diverse family united in love—cherishing each other as special and unique? *If* the world should see us living this way, then the world would know it has encountered a way of life that has the mark of Jesus upon it.

Following Jesus across cultural lines is part of God's plan for our lives . . . and essential to the realization of God's overall dream that we will grow into the likeness of the Son.

Question Ideas

1. In what ways do you see following Jesus across cultural lines as part of your new life in Him?

2. Is there a particular group of people to whom it is especially difficult for you to reach out?

3. Is your life so arranged that you simply do not have contact with people who are different from you?

4. How might you change this?

10
Spending Time with Jesus in Servanthood

Jesus was a servant. Born to serve, He lived a servant's life and stressed servanthood in His last hours on earth. While eating a farewell Passover supper with friends in a borrowed upper room, Jesus rose mid-meal to perform the task of the most humble servant in a household.

Knowing full well He was soon to be glorified (John 17), He did not hesitate to wrap a towel around His waist, take a basin in hand, and wash twelve pairs of dirty feet, saying, "Now that I, your Lord and Teacher, have washed your feet, you also should wash one another's feet. I have set you an example that you should do as I have done for you. I tell you the truth, no servant is greater than his master, nor is a messenger greater than the one who sent him. Now that you know these things, you will be blessed if you do them" (John 13:14–17).

Jesus couldn't have made it any clearer. If we want to grow in His likeness by spending time with Him, we will have to pick up the basin and find ways of washing one another's feet.

Beholding Jesus as we perform acts of servanthood is difficult for most of us. Something inherent resists the idea of becoming a servant, yet we may not even know this about ourselves until some situation tests us. As one man put it,

"We know whether or not we're servants by the way we react when we're treated like one."

It was a nippy Friday evening in November. Our friends Vicky and Sam Hines had come for supper and the four of us were gathered around the old oak table in our kitchen while a friendly fire crackled from across the room. Our conversation was jumping from one subject to another until the theme of servanthood popped up. Suddenly we became serious as we shared our common struggle to grow in this area. Then Sam, a wonderful storyteller, told us about an experience from his early years that held us captive.

SERVING FROM A BENT SPIRIT

"As I grew up in Jamaica," said Sam, "I developed a secret list of things I would not do. Even after my conversion at sixteen I preserved my list and took it with me to Bible school determined to draw a line beyond which I would not go in service to others.

"None of us as students could afford to pay for housing and boarding. If we were residents we had to work, giving our labor in exchange for the education we were receiving. We took turns cleaning the dormitory, making beds, working in the kitchen.

"I worked through these assignments without difficulty even if I thought some were beneath my dignity. But one duty proved too great a humiliation for me. One of the brothers had a bladder problem and found it necessary to use an old-fashioned chamber pot at night. Whoever was on duty in the morning was responsible to see that the pot was removed, emptied, washed, and replaced. That was asking too much! When I protested, the other students and the administration confronted me about my pride. It became quite a disruptive experience, causing me to move off campus and settle for the inconvenience of bicycling in to classes every day from my sister's house because if I didn't sleep in the dormitory, I was exempt from dormitory duty.

"But I was uneasy about my decision. I declared that I loved my brother, but emptying his chamber pot was asking too much! Things were not going well, as administrators questioned my readiness for a life of servanthood. Eventually I changed my mind and returned to residential status. I swallowed my pride and agreed to include chamber pot duty in my dorm routine. Before long the Spirit of the Lord brought me to a humble and cheerful acceptance of that particular service.

"When I look back on my spiritual pilgrimage, I thank God for bending my spirit then, so that today it is not difficult to be a servant. It is my calling to do whatever the circumstances require. Whether it be the basin and towel, or the chamber pot, or a hug of love for some unwashed, unkempt, and smelly brother, I can answer the call with joy."

I am grateful to Sam for sharing that part of his journey. It tells me that becoming a servant is a process—something we can learn with God's help! I know this is true as I watch Sam and Vicky pour their lives out for others, using their church as a base from which to serve not only their own congregation, but the growing number of homeless people in Washington. Many of us slip into the Third Street facility during the week to help serve breakfast to hundreds of homeless people, tutor the neighborhood children, or work with the Build-a-Block program. It is rare to go to Third Street and not find the Hineses there already, "washing feet" in the likeness of their Master.

BEING WITH JESUS AS HE SERVES
THE POOR AMONG US

When we study the life of our Master we find that He spent much of His life serving those we call "the disadvantaged." He cared about *all* people, yet he lived, taught, and walked primarily among the poor. It was regular folks, the "common" people as we have seen in earlier chapters, who heard Him gladly. In His first sermon He said, "The Spirit of the Lord is on me, because he has anointed me to preach good news to the poor" (Luke 4:18). And He confirmed that link with the disadvantaged when He said, "Whatever you did for one of the least of these brothers of mine, you did for Me" (Matthew 25:40).

In fact, all of Scripture is bursting with evidence that God is concerned for the poor. When we go straight to the Bible, there is no getting away from the fact that the poor are close to the very heart of God.

Surely this is one more way those of us who want to grow in His likeness need to be retrained. For the world, and much of the Christian community, would have us focus our attention (outreach, evangelism, and service) on the "important" people—men and women who are leaders, the "winners" of this world. Evangelistic crusades often have plush V.I.P. sections, and local churches sometimes defer to their prestigious members in ways that are embarrassing. Yet when He was one of us we never saw Jesus putting special emphasis on members of the Sanhedrin or the Roman government.

In contrast, many of us are uncomfortable with the poor and have arranged our lives so that we have no contact with them at all. Louie and I moved into the inner city eight years ago, in part because *we* needed to be exposed to people who were impoverished. As a friend said to me recently, "Getting involved in servanthood does more for us than it does for the people we think we are helping."

Our son Dan and his compassionate wife, Terri, echo this. Each Tuesday night they rush from their offices, often without dinner, to tutor two young people at the Third Street Church of God. Over the years, they have come to love and learn from Damon and Latrice, bright lights in a neighborhood known for darkness, crack houses, and drug-related violence. Dan gets all excited over Damon's basketball games; it's wonderful to hear the love in Latrice's voice when she calls our house trying to track down "my friend Terri." The relationships have developed into far more than a tutor-student commitment of an hour and a half together each week.

There are such rich and varied opportunities for Christians today to live out the Gospel without ever crossing a border and without being missionaries in the strict sense. Remember what St. Francis said: "Preach the gospel wherever you go; when necessary use words."

Ministries of every kind are needed in every community of our land. Think of the forgotten elderly; the minorities who long for full opportunity; the immigrants from a hundred nations struggling to survive among us; the homeless, the hungry, the stranger, the alienated, the powerless. Needs, personified in people with names and faces, are everywhere and God wants us to find them and to serve them in Jesus' name.

SERVING THE POOR—WHO DON'T LOOK POOR—AMONG US

Of course, the poor are not always the hungry or those without money or power.

Sometimes they are friends or neighbors who seem to have everything—and then in a moment of loss become as aware of their need as the poorest beggar. Desperation puts us in touch with our real condition. We are no longer too proud to reach out for what we need.

I will always remember one particular day when tragedy offered Louie an opportunity to serve two very dear friends in a simple, humble way.

It was early evening and I was putting the finishing touches on our family dinner when the phone rang. A sickening feeling clutched my stomach as I heard the desperation in the voice on the other end of the line. It was a friend from church. I could scarcely believe what he was telling me! Robbie, his son, a sensitive, intelligent, beautiful sixteen-year-old, had just shot himself and lay near death in a local hospital.

Minutes later, Louie arrived home. When he heard what had happened, he sped out the door for the hospital to be with the family. They were all together at Robbie's side when he died later that night.

What an agony! Numb with their grief, our friends had to push themselves to make the necessary arrangements that accompany such a disaster. There were papers to sign, decisions to make, and while they endured the business of death at the hospital, Louie's practical mind reflected on what must be waiting for them at home. What would it be like to return to the scene of the tragedy? Specifically, to face that blood-stained room?

Turning to Robbie's older brother Louie said, "Let's go back to the house and see if we can be of some help."

Together they washed blood from the walls and cut away the blood-soaked carpet, replacing it with a remnant they found in the garage. After several hours of work the home was restored. To Louie, it seemed a small service for grieving friends. So small, in fact, that he never mentioned it to me. But many weeks later our friends approached me at church and told me they had always loved Louie as their pastor; nothing he had ever done, however, in or out of the pulpit, had touched them as much as that act on the night of their tragedy.

The poor are also the impoverished in mind and spirit—and those whose fame or positions of power leave them wondering who their real friends are, or if they have any at all. God cares about poverty at every level.

SERVING THOSE UNDER OUR OWN ROOFS

God means for us to be servants to members of our own families. Sometimes we can do this simply by listening to heartfelt dreams. When a dream has been identified our servanthood becomes very practical and, at times, quite a struggle.

I was preparing breakfast one morning when Louie came in from jogging. He gave me a hug and I could smell the coldness of morning on him. We were living in La Jolla, California, and there was something about the damp sea air there that clung to your clothes.

Louie stretched out on the floor and began his usual

exercise routine. When I looked up from the stove, I noticed that he had stopped exercising. He was gazing out the window at a jet climbing north from Lindberg Field.

With sudden emotion and a touch of nostalgia, Louie exclaimed, "What a lucky guy! I'd sure love to do that someday. Know that, Cokey?"

I *did* know that! Through the years Louie had often talked about his desire to fly. Mother Evans told me that at age two, Louie had literally walked through his birthday cake gawking at a plane overhead. And I'd heard from his brother and sisters about his fascination with model airplanes during his growing-up years. Then in 1944, the year after we met at Hollywood High, Louie signed up for the Navy V5–V12 program, hoping to fly. But the war ended and that was that.

Then there was college, marriage, seminary, graduate school, children, and busy churches. Circumstances pushed his interest aside, but it was more than circumstances. Louie himself often questioned how flying would fit with his call to ministry. The time it would take! The expense! And even the image. I had always agreed, of course, with that kind of reasoning, and so again and again he put his dream aside.

But for me there was another, more personal reason for not encouraging Louie in his dream. I was a white-knuckle flier. I could fly to get places, but the thought of flying for pleasure was absolutely foreign to me. Picturing him flying off into the blue made my hands sweat. And there were the children. Was it fair to them for Louie to start flying?

"I'd love to fly someday, you know that?" he asked again.

Oh, yes, I knew. But I didn't much like it. So—for the second time—I didn't answer his question and I hoped somehow that the whole idea would simply go away.

And it did . . . for a while. Then one night, our dear friend Bill Gibbs, an elder in the La Jolla church, was driving Louie home from session meeting. Bill owned a flight school in San Diego. Concerned that Louie was working too hard, and knowing his passion for flying, Bill said, "Louie, now's the time. Let's get you checked out."

"Aw, Bill, I'd love to . . . but I haven't the time or the money."

"You'd better take the time, Louie; you're getting stretched out and it shows. About the money, Barbara and I want to help with that."

Some weeks later Louie was scheduled to speak at a banquet in Tucson but he hadn't read his ticket correctly and missed the flight. Dismayed because no later flight would get him there in time, he called his buddy Bill Gibbs for help. Immediately a plane and a pilot were lined up and Louie was on his way.

When he returned home late that night, I was not yet asleep. From the moment he walked into our room, I knew something was different. I have rarely seen him so excited.

"You should have seen San Diego from the air," he began. "She looked like an open jewel box, and the airport was like a Christmas tree! And this you won't believe! The pilot was a flight instructor and once we were airborne, he let me fly!"

Louie couldn't sleep all night. I had some sleepless hours myself because that night I knew I could no longer subtly stand in the way of Louie's dream. I told him that I thought he should learn to fly. Frankly, there were more sleepless nights for me in the weeks and months that followed as Louie began his flight lessons, moving happily from one certificate and rating to the next.

Not surprisingly, he took to the air naturally. A couple of

hours in the cockpit relaxed him as golf or tennis had never been able to do.

I had my own ongoing wrestling match with the Lord before I could support Louie fully in his lifelong dream. It would make a better story if I could say that some dramatic encounter totally changed my attitude—zingo! But that's not the way it was. What really happened is that over a long period of time, as I prayed for God to give me the right thoughts on the matter, the way I felt about Louie's flying simply changed. The realization that I had no right to stand in the way of the development of a God-given gift slowly dawned on me and I had peace. The emerging desire to support Louie in his dream led to our working together to save money so he could buy part-interest in a plane. With four other Christian brothers, a Bonanza 36 was purchased and it is now part of Mercy Medical Airlift, a Christian ministry that has made more than 375 flights in the last three years.

The real surprise is that I fly with Louie now. I tell him that I fly for love. Not for love of flying; I love the man who sits in the left seat of the cockpit. Except when we fly through a storm, my knuckles don't even get white anymore. Who knows, maybe someday I'll even enjoy it!

It is not always easy to support someone else's dream. This one was a struggle for me, but I needed to be stretched.

There are, of course, times when standing in support of a family member's dream is pure pleasure. One of the greatest joys Louie and I have had in our life together has been helping the four wonderful human beings entrusted to our care find the basic arena of service God has designed for each one of them.

But we have had to remind ourselves that before I gave birth to each of our children, we knew we would have them only for a season. They are not *our* children, they are God's. God called each child by name (Isaiah 49:1) and has a purpose and direction in mind for each of them. Our privilege has been to help each child discover that purpose. And there comes a time when that process is served best by standing back and allowing the principal player space and freedom to discover the way for himself or herself.

How well I remember the summer our tall, blond son Tim came home from college, weary and utterly bored with school. Not sure what he wanted to do, he felt he had to have some time off to sort things out. We knew Tim had wondrous potential (don't all parents know that about their children?), but to us, "sort out" seemed awfully close to "drop out." Yet we agreed with his decision not to return to school that year.

After a short period of "hanging around," Tim learned of an opportunity to go to India as a volunteer in mission work. The more he thought about it the more the idea appealed to him. As he explored the possibility of going, every door on which he tapped opened wide! Funds were made available from unexpected sources, plus by tightening the family belt. (Some house improvements were not made that year and Louie didn't order the new preaching robe we thought he needed.) The last obstacle to overcome was Tim's Indian visa, which he had been told was highly unlikely to come through in time for the trip. But that door, too, swung open as we received a call from the Indian Embassy the day before Tim was scheduled to leave, saying the visa was waiting to be picked up.

So Tim went on his way. Once he arrived in India he was immersed in a world that bore little resemblance to the one he had left behind. He may have turned aside from the official halls of academia for a time ("Too bad about your son, Colleen. I understand he's dropped out of school"), but a season of learning that could never be found in a textbook was waiting for him.

And the doors kept opening! Dr. and Mrs. Archie Fletcher, who headed the staff at the Wanless Hospital in Miraj, opened their home and hearts to Tim. Then the leper hospital allowed him to enter and discover a whole new world within its walls. Tim still talks about picking up lepers at the hospital gate where their fearful families had abandoned them. After carrying them inside the simple, austere facility, he would assist the Indian doctor who treated their wounds and performed corrective surgery on their limbs. Tim's letters home described the lepers as "the most grateful people in the world" for any kindness or help given them. Needless to say, those months were not only an incredible adventure, but they helped Tim discover a new depth in the meaning of service.

And, eventually, a new sense about his own life and work. This spring the whole family gathered in Rochester, New York, to "hoot and holler" with great thanksgiving as Tim graduated from medical school with his Ph.D. and M.D. degrees. We have been in his corner cheering, but the dream and the work of developing it have been his.

We can help our family members find the gifts that will help them serve others. And when the answer comes in fulfillment of a dream, then we may find our own dreams for them being fulfilled as well.

SERVING FROM LOVE

I will always remember the night Mother Teresa spoke at National Presbyterian Church. She stood before that packed congregation dressed in her muslin habit, fastened on her shoulder by a safety pin, and absolutely pierced my heart with her simplicity and spiritual power. I was about ready to pack up the family and leave for Calcutta the next day when she said something that stopped me in my tracks: "It doesn't matter whether you serve the rich or the poor, the powerful or the powerless. It is the *love* you put into the doing that matters."

That simple statement put the call upon my life into perspective. I have always felt a tug toward the poor. My heart aches with the desire to do something about the physical needs in the world around me, a world that begins just steps from my front door. As a Christian, I also ache over the spiritual poverty that certainly does not bypass the poor, but which I see most often in the eyes of people who are materially well-off among whom Louie and I have been called to serve in three different cities. Mother Teresa's words helped me understand that *the ministry is in the love.* God used her to free me to be content with my "world between two worlds" and to be willing to "bloom where I was planted."

SERVING WITH "SERPENTHOOD"

As I pour out my convictions about servanthood, I feel it is crucial to add some words of caution. Louie's brother, Bill, is a psychologist who has spent much of his professional life in counseling leaders. He says we must learn to use our "*serpent*hood" ("Be wise as serpents," Matthew 10:16) as well as our "*servant*hood." Taking Jesus as our model, we see that He did exactly that. There were times when He said no to the demands made upon Him, times when He left the crowd and got away to be alone with His Father.

Jesus looked to God for wisdom and guidance, and listened for that one voice over the roar of other voices calling for help. Sometimes that meant He did not go to those He was closest to in their time of need. He did not get to His cousin John in prison when Herod took off his head; nor did He heed the call of Mary and Martha to be with Lazarus as he lay ill and dying. He got there too late, from a human perspective. I can just see Martha pacing the floor and muttering, "Where's that Jesus when we need Him most?" But God had a greater plan by which the Son of God would receive glory by raising Lazarus from the dead (John 11:4–15).

That story was a source of comfort to me when my mother died and I was not there. God had me in another place and by the time I got to where Mother lay "ill and dying" it was too late. Humanly speaking, I failed my mother. My mourning for her was compounded by my mourning for my own failure ("She would have been there for you, you know!").

But all that was my perspective, not God's. His greater plan for me was to experience His grace, which has nothing to do with performance. Or with perfection. God reminds us again and again that His grace is sufficient for every need and there is nothing, not one blooming thing, we can do to earn it.

I love the words of Robert Farrar Capon in *Between Noon and Three* describing the rediscovery, during the Reformation, of what he calls "a whole cellar full of fifteen-hundred-year-old two-hundred-proof grace." Writes he: "The word of the Gospel, after all those centuries of trying to lift yourself into heaven by worrying about the perfection of your bootstraps, suddenly turned out to be a flat announcement that the saved were home free before they started. . . . GRACE was to be drunk neat; no water, no ice, and certainly no ginger ale; neither goodness, nor badness, nor the flowers that bloom in the spring of super-spirituality could be allowed to enter into the case."

It was that "pure, undiluted grace" that I experienced after my mother's death. With a sure conviction that life is eternal, I knew that my mother was with God and that the closer I was to God, the nearer I was to her. Now she understands everything perfectly, including how very much she was loved and why I was not there for her that last day. But God was there and that "two-hundred-proof grace" was sufficient for my mother's need in her last moments. What is more, that grace has taken away every vestige of guilt from me.

There are so many needs on so many levels. But Thomas Kelly, that wise and sensitive Quaker, was right when he said, "We cannot die on every cross." Just as Jesus looked to His Father to guide Him to His places of service, so we must learn to do the same. For the need is not always the call. We will burn out if we respond as though it is.

SERVING OUT OF GRATITUDE TO CHRIST AND A DESIRE TO BE LIKE HIM!

Why is becoming a servant so important? It is certainly not to make us appear spiritually superior. Nor is it to make us healthier psychologically—though psychiatrist Karl Menninger says this is also true. And we mustn't serve to assuage guilt or to obtain thanks, for thanks may never come.

No, the only motive worthy of real servanthood is to serve others as a way of loving and serving Jesus. "Whatever you did for one of the least of these brothers of mine, you did it for me" (Matthew 25:40).

As we become servants, we draw nearer to Jesus, and as we behold Him we grow in His likeness.

Question Ideas

1. Since Jesus was a servant-Lord, and we are to be *like* Him, what is the clear message to you about the way you are to live?

2. How can you serve family, church, friends, community without burning out?

3. In what ways did Jesus say no to people's demands on His time and energy?

4. Must you also say no sometimes? If so, how will you determine your priorities?

11

The Joy and Pain of Growing in His Likeness

I am sitting in my rocker in my study on the third floor of our old house. I often think of this as my "upper room," especially when it's early in the morning, as it is now, and there is a hush throughout the house and beyond. This is the day I have set aside to put down on paper my thoughts about the joy and pain of becoming like Jesus. And I recall that it was in another Upper Room that Jesus said, "I have told you this so that my joy may be in you and that your joy may be complete"(John 15:11). Another translation puts it this way: "I want your cup of joy to overflow."

PEOPLE OF JOY

When Jesus walked this earth, He was a Man of joy. And if you and I are growing in His likeness, we will have to make room in our lives for joy as well! He wants us to be known by our joy and to share it with the world.

But so often, this is not what the world sees in us. We laugh when we hear the story of the mother who told her child, "Wipe that smile off your face! Don't you know you're in church?" But it's really no joke! Too often Christians are known not for their gladness and joy, but for their *lack* of it!

C. S. Lewis put it masterfully in a letter to Sheldon Vanauken, quoted in *A Severe Mercy*, when he wrote, "The best argument for Christianity is Christians—their joy, their completeness. But the strongest argument against Christianity is also Christians—when they are somber and joyless, narrow and repressive. Then Christianity dies a thousand deaths!"

Another great advocate for joy was the apostle Paul. He spoke about it in almost all his letters as though he took for granted the fact that the early Church was to be a community of joy. In his letter to the church in Philippi, he wrote: "Rejoice in the Lord always. I will say it again: Rejoice!" And again and again he said it: fourteen times in that one short book! No wonder scholars call Philippians the "Epistle of Joy"!

Joy is a fruit of the Spirit (see Galatians 5:22). In other words, when we open ourselves to Christ and He enters our lives through the Holy Spirit, we become daughters or sons of God. Joy, then, is our birthright. We cannot earn that joy or work it up within ourselves. It is ours through the Spirit of the One who loved us and gave Himself for us.

When He enters our lives, joy comes with Him! I like the little poster that declares, "Joy is the banner that waves above the castle to show that the King is in residence." Throughout the life of the Church, joy has been the benchmark of true believers. Starting with Jesus, Paul, the early Church, and down through the years, this has been so.

• St. Francis and his little brothers were called "the merry band."

• Blaise Pascal had a note sewn into his coat pocket, found after his death, that witnessed to his deeply mystical experience of "joy, unspeakable joy."

• Jonathan Edwards in the eighteenth century wrote that

joy was central to the list of characteristics that separated those with a genuine Christian experience from "religious counterfeits."

• Pope John the 23rd preached that "joy is the infallible proof that God is in a person's life."

• Mother Teresa and her Sisters of Charity who serve the dying in Calcutta are called "the happiest of people."

I get carried away with this subject! St. Francis de Sales summed it all up when he said, "A sad saint is a *sad* sort of saint!"

But there are many "sad saints" among us, aren't there?

And I often wonder why this is so. Perhaps, as our friend Sam Hines puts it, it is because "there are so many religious people who are not yet spiritual." Or, to put it another way, many who go to church have not appropriated the good news for their own lives. And all the while the Holy Spirit is waiting to convince us that we *are* children of God; that Christ wants to live in us, and that He loves us more than we can ever comprehend. That is the Spirit's task and when we ask and allow Him to do that for us, then joy is our gift. Joy is a fruit of the Spirit. Believe it! It is a prerequisite for growing in His likeness!

But again—why do so many refuse this lovely gift?

JOY-ROBBERS

Some time ago I read a delightful article on "killjoys" by Doris Donnelly. She suggested that there are some "sad saints" around because they have yielded to the "killjoys" of this world: those who have practiced and become skillful in undermining the faith from which joy springs. The world is full of them and, what is more, there has never been a shortage of people who scoff at joy!

Surely Jesus must have known a few killjoys. Remember the people who asked, "Who is this man who goes to parties and weddings? This friend of publicans and sinners?" And then there were those who got after Him for not living an outwardly pious life, as did the ascetics who were followers of His cousin John. It was the religious people of His day who had the biggest problem with the joyous freedom of Jesus.

But the Gospels make it clear that Jesus didn't give in to the killjoys. He never denied His joy nor did He feel the need to justify it. He simply lived it, owned it, gave it away ("My joy I give to you"), and told His disciples repeatedly that He wanted them to share it with others. So, in His likeness, we would do well to resist the joy-robbers who still shoot their arrows.

But it isn't only other people who kill our joy. We do it to ourselves. We rob ourselves of the gift of joy God means for us to have and we do it by becoming anxious about our lives.

We forget that anxiety is sin—very respectable and commonly practiced, to be sure, but nevertheless sin. When we wring our hands anxiously, we are *not* trusting God.

Too many of us allow remorse over yesterday and anxiety about tomorrow to rob us of today. The Scottish author George MacDonald wrote:

> No one ever sank under the burden of the day. It is when tomorrow's burden is added to the burden of today that the weight is more than one can bear. Never load yourself so. If you find yourself so loaded, at least remember this: it is your own doing, not God's. He *begs* you to leave the future to Him, and mind the present.

Joy is for *now*. This is the day the Lord has made. This is the day in which we will rejoice and be glad!

Louie and I were in our seats in the theatre at Princeton Seminary where our son Jamie was to play one of the leading roles in Thornton Wilder's *Our Town*. As we sat in the dimly lit auditorium, my thoughts drifted back through the past twenty years of Jamie's life.

Jamie had been born dyslexic and hyperkinetic. Large, happy, gregarious, he was always a joy *and* a terrific handful. Incredibly bright, as dyslexics *often* are, he had an eagerness for life and a tenderness of heart that made him a most wonderful and unusual human being. When he went to school, he began to realize something was different for him, yet he met head-on the dyslexic's heartbreaking struggle with reading, writing, and learning. Meanwhile, Louie and I were experiencing the pain and anger parents of learning-disabled children feel when the child they love comes home from school asking, "Mommy, why do the kids call me 'Dummy-dummy Evans'?" And, of course, there were the emotional wounds that go with that!

We spent years praying, working, and searching for the right help for Jamie. But somewhere along the way *he* made up his own mind that with his "friend-God's" help, he was going to make it. (For the full story read *An Uncommon Gift* by James Steward Evans).

Jamie's doctor warned him—and us—that everything would be twice as hard for our son. And it was. Tutoring after school, repeating classes, going to school on Saturday to work with the English professor (God, thank You for Dr. Ruge!), coaching in speech to overcome a not uncommon dyslexic stutter, marking a big "L" and "R" on the thigh pads of his football uniform to avoid running the wrong direction, and going off to college and taking Greek twice in order to pass it once in seminary. The doctor who said that everything would be difficult for Jamie was right. But he also said he would make it—and indeed he did! Jamie was presently in his middle year at seminary.

All the folding chairs in the theatre were filled now, and a few students were standing around the sides of the room. The house was dark, the curtain went up, and the play began.

It was a good production. Jamie as George and his female counterpart, Elsie Armstrong, who played the part of Emily, were doing a terrific job. At the end of Act One, Louie and I were both choked up because Jamie had gotten through his lines without one stammer. I'm sure the people around us didn't understand why we were so emotional, but we didn't mind.

The play continued and, if you are familiar with *Our Town,* you will remember that Emily dies in childbirth. Then after her death, there is a scene that absolutely nailed me as it unfolded. This one scene is my reason for sharing this tale and I ask Thornton Wilder's forgiveness in advance for the mistakes I'm sure to make as I retell this strictly from memory.

Emily is in heaven, but she longs to be back on earth one more time with those she loves. She begs the stage manager to permit her to return for a single day. He tries his best to dissuade her, but finally gives in to her desire to go back and relive her twelfth birthday. Heaven fades and when the lights go up we see twelve-year-old Emily in her family kitchen. She stands in the middle of the room, awed by everything around her. Her mother is rushing around the kitchen fixing breakfast, mixing a birthday cake—busy, busy, busy! Emily tries to get her attention, but she is pushed aside. Again Emily tries— "Mother, I want to talk to you"— but her mother is too caught up in all she has to do to stop and talk. Finally, in exasperation, Emily shouts, "Mama,

Mama, stop! Will you look at me just one minute as though you *really see me?*"

But she can't.

Emily's mother—like so many of us—is too busy to look and *really see* her daughter on her twelfth birthday. At the conclusion of the day, dazzled by the beauty of everything around her and pained by how unaware people are of life, Emily cries out in despair, "Oh, you are too wonderful for anyone to realize." Later that night, she returns to the graveyard, sad and distraught. Looking at the stage manager with tears in her eyes, she asks, "Do human beings ever *realize life* as they live it?"

He thinks for a moment, then replies, "No. Poets and saints, maybe. But, no, human beings do *not* realize life as they live it."

Though the play continued, it was over for me. I simply kept hearing those words—"Realize life as you live it"—and I knew the message was for me.

JOY IS FOR NOW

This is the day; *now* is the time; whatever the circumstance. *Colleen, don't put off realizing life as you live it.*

O Lord, burn that into my heart.

Now, now, now. Life and joy are to be experienced *now* because *now* is where He is and if we are to behold Him and grow in His likeness, we must do it *now.*

Since that night of the play I have consciously tried to take joy in the Lord *now,* not tomorrow, or even later today, but *now.* And I have tried to be more aware of the beauty of the world, particularly the *people* in my world—to look and *really see* them, to take time to appreciate them. Now, no matter what!

I'll never forget the afternoon I went to Louie's study just to tell him he brought me joy. I stood at the open door and, without warning, announced, "Louie Evans, have I ever told you how much joy you bring to my life?" He looked up, took off his Ben Franklin glasses, pushed back his desk chair, motioned me over to his side, and, gathering me into his lap, gave me an enormous hug. It was some reaction!

Then he said, "In all the years of our marriage, I don't believe you have ever said that to me."

I could hardly believe what I was hearing! Louie was the one who first shared Christ with me in a way I could understand, the one who had shared his life with me on the deepest level all these years, and I'd never told him he brought me joy? *Shame on me!*

I've tried to make up for that in the years since, not only with Louie, but with all my family and friends as well.

Saint Paul lived out his joy. Remember when he said to his friends in Philippi, "I thank my God every time I remember you. In all my prayers for all of you, I always pray with joy" (Philippians 1:3–4). But Paul's deepest joy was in his relationship with Christ. And so it should be for us. In fact, it is *Christ in us* who frees us to take joy in people.

Christians who know they are loved and forgiven are the merriest people in the world. They know how to celebrate the *now!* Louie and I often comment that our most relaxing, hilarious times are spent with our covenant brothers and sisters in Christ because they are so free and so "springloaded" for fun!

Growing in the likeness of Jesus means our capacity for genuine, abandoned enjoyment increases. But that isn't all. Life in Christ is not simply freedom and mirth.

JOY IS NOT THE ABSENCE OF PAIN

It is also, at times, an agony, because joy is not the absence of pain; it is the presence of God through every circumstance of life, *including* pain. And, contrary to much that is taught today, Christians are not immune from pain and suffering. The "name your pleasure, claim your treasure" philosophy would have us believe otherwise, but it is a lie. As Lewis Smedes has said, "Christians do not live in a sanctified pleasure-dome."

In fact, because we are Christians, we care more and so we will hurt more than other people. As much as God means for us to enjoy life, we must never confuse the joy of Jesus Christ with prosperity, pleasure, and fun. Nor is it happiness, for *happy* comes from the root word for "happening," which implies that happiness depends on circumstances. These may or may not coexist with joy, but they are *not* His joy.

The joy Jesus called "My joy" is so deep, so dependent on our relationship with God, that it is untouched by "happenings" or by the various struggles, trials, and painful experiences every one of us will encounter in this life.

I suppose because of my love for the sea, I think of Christ's joy as a treasure hidden in the ocean floor of my life ... untouched by the storm that may be raging on the surface of the sea.

One morning I was sipping a cup of coffee and looking through *The Washington Post* when my eyes were drawn to an article about a couple we know, not intimately, but well enough to care about deeply. They had come to Washington to take a place of leadership in the administration and, as warm, genuine Christians, had won the hearts of all of us who had the chance to know them. Reading the article, I was

stunned by the news that their teenage daughter had died
suddenly from a mysterious illness. The anguish of their
loss welled up within me. I could well imagine the pain they
were experiencing at that moment, so I did the only thing
I know to do at such times: I prayed. And I wept.

Later in the day, remembering words I had read somewhere, "A letter is a prayer that meant what it said," I went
to my desk and penned a note to our friends. And almost
by return mail, a card came back to me, bearing a message
so simple yet so powerful that I will never forget it.

"Dear Colleen—Thank you for your prayers. Our hearts
are breaking, but we have the joy of Jesus. Isabelle."

It was that same uncommon joy I witnessed in the life of
Mother Evans. Louie's father had just died, after almost
sixty years of marriage to his wonderful Marie. To our
amazement Mother Evans seemed filled with joy. One
morning we found her in the driveway in front of the house,
dressed in her blue jeans and tennis shoes, washing her car.
With her eyes dancing she told us, "All my married life, I've
asked God to allow me the privilege of taking care of my
Louie to the very end. The dear Lord granted my prayer!
Then this morning when I woke, I thought of Louie in the
company of the Lord, and I was filled with such an awareness of God's presence!" Looking at her oldest son she
asked, "Do you think I should hide my gratitude and joy?"

"Mom," Louie replied, "that's what the ministry of the
Holy Spirit is all about. You *know* where Daddy is. He's with
the Lord! He's more alive now than ever before. Just think
how he's rejoicing right now, so why shouldn't we be joyful,
too, even in the midst of our tears?"

And that's exactly what she chose to do. At the memorial
service she wore a white tailored suit. It was a day of celebration and she was dressed for the occasion. She went

through her entire mourning with vitality and grace, exclaiming periodically, "Oh, how good God is! Thank You, dear Lord." And in all the years since Louie's father died, Mother Evans has been an example of someone growing in the likeness of her Lord. At 93, she lives by herself and, in spite of failing eyesight, walks a mile a day with a friend, does her own housework, and cooks her own simple meals. Recently during one of our frequent phone visits, she asked, "By the way, Cokey, have I told you that I have a full-time job these days? I take care of a little old lady from Pasadena, and she's a handful! Takes all my time!"

And always she has a grateful attitude toward the Lord. I suspect that her thankful heart holds the secret of her joy.

Mother Evans reminds me that painful, difficult circumstances come to all people, and while we cannot choose our circumstances, we can—and do—choose our attitudes. And she has consistently chosen the attitude of gratitude, praise, and joy.

SUFFERING: A STUBBORN FACT OF LIFE

Suffering comes to all of us, a stubborn fact of life. To be convinced of this we need simply to look at Jesus. He suffered beyond anything you and I could imagine. And it was not only death on a cross, it was also the rejection and betrayal He knew in life.

If *He* had to suffer those hurts, no one is immune. Suffering, deserved and undeserved, is simply part of the human predicament. There are so many levels of suffering. Some come simply because we live in a world where natural disasters occur. I have witnessed the pain of famine as I have visited World Vision relief projects around the word. None of us escapes knowing about floods, earthquakes, wind, and fire in our televised world.

But our world is also imperfect because *we* have infected it with our sin. Natural disaster pales alongside human disasters, which have their own particular horror. We kill one another in wars, in gas chambers, and on the streets where we live. One evening I was sitting in my study when I heard a volley of . . . what was it? Backfire, sharp explosions, or (I dreaded the thought) gunshots? Minutes later, sirens confirmed my fear. The volley had been shots—and close! *O God, what is going on?*

The ten o'clock news told me. "This story is just in. . . ." Three young men shot in their car. No names released. Gang-type execution. Drug-related. The news team is on the scene. The camera zooms in on three young women, sobbing as neighbors try to comfort them. They watch as the bodies of their dead sons are lifted onto gurneys and carried off by ambulances to the city morgue. And all this happens a short distance from where I sit. *O God, help us.* Our world is imperfect, sinful, and dangerous. And so much of it is our own doing, our own mistakes, our own callous thoughtlessness. Yet we continue to blame God.

How often I hear, "How could a God of love allow that?" God gets blamed for so much that the Bible specifically warns against!

I came across excerpts recently in *Life-Rails: Holding Fast to God's Promises*, by Scott Walker, from a moving sermon preached by Dr. William Sloane Coffin, Jr. It was delivered just days after his son died when his car skidded into Boston Harbor. In the sermon, Dr. Coffin shared a conversation he had had with someone who tried to tell him his son's death was "within the will of God." Dr. Coffin replied courageously,

Do you think it was the will of God that Alex never fixed that lousy windshield wiper of his, that he was probably driving too fast in such a storm, that he probably had had a couple of "frosties" too many? Do you think that it is God's will that there are no street lights along that stretch of road, and no guard rail separating the road and Boston Harbor? When will people get it through their heads that God doesn't go around this world with His finger on triggers, His fist around knives, His hands on steering wheels? God is dead set against all unnatural death.

Yes, we all suffer, sometimes as innocent victims of natural disasters, sometimes as innocent victims of human disasters resulting from the sins of others, and sometimes with no one to blame but ourselves.

And through it all, what difference does our faith make? Surely it sustains us, but it does not save or shield us from suffering. (Read 2 Corinthians 11:24–28 for a list of some of the things Paul suffered even though—and in many cases *because*—he was a man of faith.)

SUFFERING: A MEANS OF GROWTH

How does suffering affect our growth toward the likeness of Jesus? The answer to this question is so crucial to our journey that it leads us, in my opinion, to very holy ground. Listen carefully with heart and mind to what our Lord Himself clearly says to us:

"If the world hates you, keep in mind that it hated me first. If you belonged to the world, it would love you as its own. As it is, you do not belong to the world, but I have chosen you out of the world. That is why the world hates you. Remember the words I spoke to you: 'No servant is greater than his master.' If they persecuted me, they will persecute you also. . . . They will treat you this way be-

cause of my name, for they do not know the One who sent me."
                                                    John 15:18–21

"Anyone who does not take his cross and follow me is not worthy
of me."   Matthew 10:38

Clearly our Lord is saying we cannot "be like the Master"
if we are not willing to suffer with Him and for Him. We
must be willing to pick up our particular cross and follow
Him into an arena where people really do get hurt and are
sometimes crucified. Growing in the likeness of Jesus will
mean joy, but it will also mean doing battle with the forces
of evil in this world. And when we fight evil, evil fights back!

The great promise is that God will work actively in our
lives to transform tragedy into victory, absurdity into mean-
ingfulness, pain and tears into joy and laughter. He will take
us from the cross of "Good" Friday to the resurrection of
Easter morn. Of course, the journey from Golgotha to the
empty tomb will take time and patience. We will surely
stumble and fall along the way, but in the process we will
grow.

Remember the counsel James, the brother of the Lord,
has given to us: "Count it all joy . . . when you meet various
trials, for you know that the testing of your faith produces
steadfastness. And let steadfastness have its full effect, that
you may be perfect and complete, lacking in nothing"
(James 1:2–4, rsv).

As I sit in my writing chair lost in thought, the memory
of the last Congressional election floods my mind and I
think of two of our close covenant friends. Don and Carolyn
Bonker want more than anything to serve Christ in all they
do. About a year ago, after months of prayer, Don felt led
to give up a secure seat as a U.S. Representative from the

state of Washington to run for the U.S. Senate. He was the underdog in the race, but he, Carolyn, and their incredibly loyal and enthusiastic support team ran a great campaign and the polls showed Don gaining steadily week by week. The night of the election, we were as excited as the staff and kept getting progress reports from the Washington, D.C., office and the state. It was nip-and-tuck, but as the night wore on, it became clear that barring a miracle in Seattle, where the greatest population lived and where Don was least known, he was going to lose the election.

At about four in the morning Eastern Standard Time, our son Dan, who was with Don on the West Coast, called. His voice was choked with emotion as he said, "Don just gave his concession speech. What an inspiration to see a Christian public servant look beyond personal defeat to serving God in larger ways." Then his voice broke. "I've never been so proud of Don."

Some of us were at National Airport to meet the Bonkers when they returned to D.C., offering expressions of love and pride. Seven-year-old Jonathan Bonker returned to school and announced, "My daddy is out of work." That condition didn't last long. Don was offered a new and exciting opportunity in the private sector and none of us believes that is the end of Don's *public* service. In the meantime, God is building new strengths into the Bonkers' lives through the pain of losing an election. Carolyn expresses it eloquently when she says:

"It's been a difficult yet precious time to see Don go through this crucible. First the pressure and fire of the campaign, and then the ramifications of loss, as if the Lord were refining and removing slack materials through this experience.

"But there were sweet moments as well. After the election, Don was speaking on behalf of the party. When he walked into the packed hall, the audience gave him a standing ovation. He was grateful that God had allowed him that honor even in the midst of defeat. For all through the campaign, his prayer had been, 'God, give me humility in victory and grace in defeat.' "

Ernest Hemingway wrote, "The world breaks everyone and afterward, many are strong at the broken places." This is surely what is in process in the lives of Don and Carolyn Bonker. And as I watch them grow through this difficult season, I am reminded that God can heal any broken thing when we offer up all the pieces.

SUFFERING: A MINISTRY TO OTHERS

Another way God uses our suffering is as a bridge of ministry to others. "Praise be to . . . God . . . who comforts us in all our troubles, so that we can comfort those in any trouble with the comfort we ourselves have received from God" (2 Corinthians 1:3–4).

How true it is that until we walk in someone else's shoes, we simply do not know what the pinched toe feels like! I think of a senator who has recently been the innocent victim of a fiery trial. From the onset to the vindicating resolution of that trial, he has carried a 3" × 5" card with the names of other hurting people going through their own trials. The card, carried next to his heart, reminds him to call those people and to hold them in his prayers. He is actively comforting people with the comfort he has received from God.

I'm also reminded of our good friends Kathy and Dun. In the sixth month of Kathy's pregnancy, she lost the baby they had prayed for for so long. Kathy was barely home from the hospital when she ran to the bedside of another young mother-to-be in our church who was experiencing the same agonizing loss. Kathy could comfort her. She understood.

I recall the new empathy I felt with those going into surgery once I experienced major surgery myself. I no longer wondered at their need for ministry, for I remember the battle I waged with fear when the doctor said, "Colleen, it may not be anything, but I simply can't be sure until we operate." God uses those moments to sensitize us forever to the needs of others.

SUFFERING: A WAY OF IDENTIFYING WITH CHRIST

Peter alludes to one more way God uses suffering when he says, "Dear friends, do not be surprised at the painful trial you are suffering, as though something strange were happening to you. But rejoice that you participate in the sufferings of Christ, so that you may be overjoyed when his glory is revealed. . . . If you suffer as a Christian, do not be ashamed, but praise God that you bear that name" (1 Peter 4:12–13, 16).

When suffering identifies us with Christ and honors Him, that is the highest purpose our pain and suffering can ever serve. At that moment, we should "praise God that we bear that name."

But too often this is not our response. Too often we are surprised by suffering and we *do* think it strange. "Why does she have to suffer when she's such a good person?" "What did I ever do to deserve this?"

I began this book by saying I was writing from my own need and out of my own desire to grow in the likeness of

Jesus. In no part of this study has my life been more stretched than at this very point. If suffering is an inescapable part of being transformed into the likeness of my Master, and He said it is, then I must stop asking why God's people suffer and begin asking, "Jesus, if I am Your disciple, show me how this suffering can transform me."

In these days of study I have begun to ask myself, "Is the salt of my life so saltless, and the light of my life so dim, that people cannot see any evidence that I am growing in the likeness of my Lord?"

SUFFERING: A SIGN OF GROWING IN HIS LIKENESS

It is a tough question and it has pushed me to a new place. Not that I am eager to suffer; that would be unhealthy. But when it comes, we are not to be surprised as though something strange were happening to us. We are to pick up our crosses and follow Jesus, knowing full well He does not walk a rose-strewn path. We are willing to suffer and to count it a privilege to be identified with Him in our suffering as we continue to grow in His likeness.

I have to stop and I cannot think of a better way to do so than through the words of Amy Carmichael, who speaks so much more eloquently than I ever could.

> Hast thou no scar?
> No hidden scar on foot, or side, or hand?
> I hear thee sung as mighty in the land,
> I hear them hail thy bright, ascendant star,
> Hast thou no scar?
>
> Hast thou no wound?
> Yet I was wounded by the archers, spent,

n no part of this study has my life been more
d than at this very point. If suffering is an inescap-
t of being transformed into the likeness of my
nd He said it is, then I must stop asking why God's
ffer and begin asking, "Jesus, if I am Your disciple,
how this suffering can transform me."
e days of study I have begun to ask myself, "Is the
life so saltless, and the light of my life so dim, that
nnot see any evidence that I am growing in the
 my Lord?"

FERING: A SIGN OF GROWING
IN HIS LIKENESS

h question and it has pushed me to a new place.
 eager to suffer; that would be unhealthy. But
s, we are not to be surprised as though some-
 were happening to us. We are to pick up our
llow Jesus, knowing full well He does not walk
 path. We are willing to suffer and to count it
 be identified with Him in our suffering as we
ow in His likeness.
p and I cannot think of a better way to do so
he words of Amy Carmichael, who speaks so
quently than I ever could.

 scar?
ar on foot, or side, or hand?
ung as mighty in the land,
ail thy bright, ascendant star,
 scar?

 wound?
nded by the archers, spent,

---

state of Washington to run for the U.S. Senate. He was the underdog in the race, but he, Carolyn, and their incredibly loyal and enthusiastic support team ran a great campaign and the polls showed Don gaining steadily week by week. The night of the election, we were as excited as the staff and kept getting progress reports from the Washington, D.C., office and the state. It was nip-and-tuck, but as the night wore on, it became clear that barring a miracle in Seattle, where the greatest population lived and where Don was least known, he was going to lose the election.

At about four in the morning Eastern Standard Time, our son Dan, who was with Don on the West Coast, called. His voice was choked with emotion as he said, "Don just gave his concession speech. What an inspiration to see a Christian public servant look beyond personal defeat to serving God in larger ways." Then his voice broke. "I've never been so proud of Don."

Some of us were at National Airport to meet the Bonkers when they returned to D.C., offering expressions of love and pride. Seven-year-old Jonathan Bonker returned to school and announced, "My daddy is out of work." That condition didn't last long. Don was offered a new and exciting opportunity in the private sector and none of us believes that is the end of Don's *public* service. In the meantime, God is building new strengths into the Bonkers' lives through the pain of losing an election. Carolyn expresses it eloquently when she says:

"It's been a difficult yet precious time to see Don go through this crucible. First the pressure and fire of the campaign, and then the ramifications of loss, as if the Lord were refining and removing slack materials through this experience.

"But there were sweet moments as well. After the election, Don was speaking on behalf of the party. When he walked into the packed hall, the audience gave him a standing ovation. He was grateful that God had allowed him that honor even in the midst of defeat. For all through the campaign, his prayer had been, 'God, give me humility in victory and grace in defeat.' "

Ernest Hemingway wrote, "The world breaks everyone and afterward, many are strong at the broken places." This is surely what is in process in the lives of Don and Carolyn Bonker. And as I watch them grow through this difficult season, I am reminded that God can heal any broken thing when we offer up all the pieces.

SUFFERING: A MINISTRY TO OTHERS

Another way God uses our suffering is as a bridge of ministry to others. "Praise be to . . . God . . . who comforts us in all our troubles, so that we can comfort those in any trouble with the comfort we ourselves have received from God" (2 Corinthians 1:3–4).

How true it is that until we walk in someone else's shoes, we simply do not know what the pinched toe feels like! I think of a senator who has recently been the innocent victim of a fiery trial. From the onset to the vindicating resolution of that trial, he has carried a 3″ × 5″ card with the names of other hurting people going through their own trials. The card, carried next to his heart, reminds him to call those people and to hold them in his prayers. He is actively comforting people with the comfort he has received from God.

I'm also reminded of our good friends Kathy and Dun. In the sixth month of Kathy's pregnancy, she lost the baby they had prayed for for so long. Kathy was barely home

Leaned Me against a tree to die; and rent
By ravening beasts that compassed Me, I swooned:
Hast *thou* no wound?

No wound? No scar?
Yet, as the Master shall the servant be,
And, piercèd are the feet that follow Me;
But thine are whole: can he have followed far
Who has nor wound nor scar?*

Yes, "as the Master shall the servant be"—scars and all. That is our quest and that is God's great dream for our lives. The road Jesus traveled and would have us travel after Him is not *ultimately* a road of suffering. It is a road *to joy* that indeed passes through suffering. But suffering is not its final destination. The Gospel is not the Gospel without the cross, but the Gospel doesn't end with the cross. There is a resurrection day! And it was because of "the joy set before him [that Jesus] endured the cross" (Hebrews 12:2).

Jesus said, "In the world ye shall have tribulation: but be of good cheer; I have overcome the world" (John 16:33, KJV). I cannot imagine a greater cause for joy than that! Of course there will be suffering. But let's remember that Christ, who lives in us through the Holy Spirit, is an overcomer. He is asking us to reflect His "good cheer" to a cheerless world as we continue our lifelong journey of growing in His likeness.

Question Ideas

1.   Does being a disciple of Christ mean you will always be happy?

---

* From *Toward Jerusalem* by Amy Carmichael © 1936 Dohnavur Fellowship, Fort Wayne, Pa.: Christian Literature Crusade. Used by permission.

2. Describe in your own words the difference between happiness and the joy of Jesus.

3. When have you experienced pain and joy coexisting in your life?

4. Does suffering mean you have done something wrong? Could it mean you have done something right? Explain.

5. Becoming like the Master means following Him through pain into joy. Do you believe it? Will you receive His joy—now?